ELEGY

Elegy is the public display of private grief, but in an age of televised funerals and visible bereavement, such displays of mourning take on different meanings through being open to public scrutiny.

Providing an overview of the history of elegy and the different ways in which the term is used, David Kennedy:

- Outlines the origins and key characteristics of canonical and modern elegy.
- Provides close readings of texts including early English elegies, the elegies of Tennyson, Arnold and Hardy, AIDS and breast-cancer elegies, contemporary poetry and film.
- Examines the psychology and cultural background underlying works of mourning, introducing the theories of Freud, Lacan and Derrida.
- Surveys the latest critical approaches, the diffusion of elegy beyond poetry into contemporary writing and how it has been adapted post-9/11.

Emphasizing and explaining the significance of elegy today, this illuminating guide to an emotive literary genre will be of interest to students of literature, media and culture.

David Kennedy is Senior Lecturer in Creative Writing at the University of Hull. He is the editor of *Necessary Steps: Poetry, Elegy, Walking, Spirit*; and publishes widely on contemporary poetry.

THE NEW CRITICAL IDIOM

SERIES EDITOR: JOHN DRAKAKIS, UNIVERSITY OF STIRLING

The New Critical Idiom is an invaluable series of introductory guides to today's critical terminology. Each book:

- provides a handy, explanatory guide to the use (and abuse) of the term
- offers an original and distinctive overview by a leading literary and cultural critic
- relates the term to the larger field of cultural representation

With a strong emphasis on clarity, lively debate and the widest possible breadth of examples, *The New Critical Idiom* is an indispensable approach to key topics in literary studies.

Also available in this series:

ELEGY

David Kennedy

Routledge
Taylor & Francis Group

LONDON AND NEW YORK

First published 2007 by Routledge
2 Park Square, Milton Park, Abingdon, Oxon OX14 4RN

Simultaneously published in the USA and Canada
by Routledge
270 Madison Ave, New York, NY 10016

Routledge is an imprint of the Taylor & Francis Group, an informa business

Typeset in Garamond and Scala Sans by Taylor & Francis Books
Printed and bound in Great Britain by
TJ International Ltd, Padstow, Cornwall

British Library Cataloguing in Publication Data
A catalogue record for this book is available from the British Library

Library of Congress Cataloging in Publication Data
Library of Congress Cataloging-in-Publication Data
Kennedy, David, 1959-
     Elegy / David Kennedy.
          p. cm. – (The new critical idiom)
     Includes bibliographical references and index.
ISBN 978-0-415-36776-9 (hardback : alk. paper) – ISBN 978-0-415-36777-6
(pbk. : alk. paper) – ISBN 978-0-203-01999-3 (ebook) 1. Elegiac poetry,
English–History and criticism. 2. Literary form–History. 3. Mourning
customs in literature. 4. Grief in literature. 5. Funeral rites and
ceremonies in literature. 6. Death in literature. I. Title.
     PR509.E4K46 2007
     821'.0409–dc22

                              2007011783

ISBN 10: 0-415-36776-X (hbk)
ISBN 10: 0-415-36777-8 (pbk)
ISBN 10: 0-203-01999-7 (ebk)

ISBN 13: 978-0-415-36776-9 (hbk)
ISBN 13: 978-0-415-36777-6 (pbk)
ISBN 13: 978-0-203-01999-3 (ebk)

For Christine

CONTENTS

SERIES EDITOR'S PREFACE

The New Critical Idiom is a series of introductory books which seeks to extend the lexicon of literary terms, in order to address the radical changes which have taken place in the study of literature during the last decades of the twentieth century. The aim is to provide clear, well-illustrated accounts of the full range of terminology currently in use, and to evolve histories of its changing usage.

The current state of the discipline of literary studies is one where there is considerable debate concerning basic questions of terminology. This involves, among other things, the boundaries which distinguish the literary from the non-literary; the position of literature within the larger sphere of culture; the relationship between literatures of different cultures; and questions concerning the relation of literary to other cultural forms within the context of interdisciplinary studies.

It is clear that the field of literary criticism and theory is a dynamic and heterogeneous one. The present need is for individual volumes on terms which combine clarity of exposition with an adventurousness of perspective and a breadth of application. Each volume will contain as part of its apparatus some indication of the direction in which the definition of particular terms is likely to move, as well as expanding the disciplinary boundaries within which some of these terms have been traditionally contained. This will involve some re-situation of terms within the larger field of cultural representation, and will introduce examples from the area of film and the modern media in addition to examples from a variety of literary texts.

ACKNOWLEDGEMENTS

My thanks are due to Professor John Drakakis for commissioning a proposal for this book and for detailed feedback on the manuscript; and to Terry Gifford for first suggesting I write the book and make the approach.

The book was written during an AHRC Fellowship in Creative & Performing Arts 2004–7 entitled 'Reviving Elegy: Towards a distinct contemporary poetry of private and public mourning'. Professor Peter Middleton of the University of Southampton set the project in motion with discussions and materials. The English Department at Leeds Trinity & All Saints was a generous host. I received tremendous support from the whole English team at Leeds Trinity but I am particularly indebted to Paul Hardwick for directing me to Chaucer's 'Book of the Duchess'; to Amina Alyal for directing me to the many references to unmanly tears in Shakespeare; and to Jane de Gay for drawing my attention to the passage from Virginia Woolf's diaries which begins the book.

Cliff Forshaw discussed the project with me at some length, read several chapters and made valuable suggestions.

Alan Halsey kindly let me consult generally unavailable volumes by Coleridge and Shenstone.

Christopher Noble allowed me to quote from his online doctoral thesis on Victorian elegy; and Kate Lilley allowed me to quote from her unpublished doctoral thesis on masculine elegy.

My wife, Christine, deserves special thanks for her support and encouragement throughout the writing of the book.

The author and publishers would like to thank the following for permission to use their work:

'In Memory of Sigmund Freud', copyright 1940 and renewed 1968 by W. H. Auden, 'In Memory of W. B. Yeats', copyright 1940 and renewed 1968 by W. H. Auden, from *Collected Poems* by W. H. Auden. Used by permission of Random House, Inc.

Excerpts from 'A Procession at Candlemas' from *Collected Poems* by Amy Clampitt. Reprinted by permission of Faber and Faber Ltd and A. A. Knopf, New York.

Carcanet for John Ash's *Two Books* (2002).

'Crossroads in the Past' from *Your Name Here*. Copyright © 2000 by John Ashbery. Reprinted by permission of Carcanet and Georges Borchardt, Inc., for the author.

Faber and Faber Ltd, for excerpts from W. H. Auden's 'In Memory of Sigmund Freud' and 'In Memory of W. B. Yeats'.

Excerpts from *My Alexandria* by Mark Doty published by Jonathan Cape reprinted by permission of The Random House Group Ltd and The University of Illinois Press. Excerpts from *Source* by Mark Doty published by Jonathan Cape reprinted by permission of The Random House Group Ltd, Mark Doty and The Robbins Office, New York.

Excerpts from *Collected Poems* (1993) and *Boss Cupid* (2000) by Thom Gunn. Reprinted by permission of Faber and Faber Ltd and Farrar, Straus & Giroux, LLC.

Excerpts from 'Against Elegies', 'Corona', 'Letter to Julie in a New Decade', 'Year's End', 'Cancer Winter', 'August Journal', from *Winter Numbers* by Marilyn Hacker. Copyright ©1994 by Marilyn Hacker. Used by permission of the author, Frances Collin, Literary Agent and W. W. Norton & Company, Inc.

Excerpts from *Field Work* (1979) by Seamus Heaney. Copyright © 1979 Seamus Heaney. Reprinted by permission of Faber and Faber Ltd and Farrar, Straus & Giroux, LLC.

Carcanet for excerpts from Patrick McGuinness's translation of Mallarmé *For Anatole's Tomb* (2003).

Sean O'Brien for 'A Coffin Boat'.

The lines from 'Power'. Copyright © 2002 by Adrienne Rich. Copyright © 1978 by W. W. Norton & Company, Inc., the lines from 'A Woman Dead in her Forties'. Copyright © 2002 by Adrienne Rich. Copyright © 1978 by W. W. Norton & Company, Inc. From *The Dream of a Common Language: Poems 1974–1977* by Adrienne Rich. Used by permission of the author and W. W. Norton & Company, Inc.

Excerpts from Dylan Thomas's 'A Refusal to Mourn the Death, by Fire, of a Child in London' from *The Poems of Dylan Thomas*,

1

FORM WITHOUT FRONTIERS

In a diary entry for 27 June 1925, Virginia Woolf wrote 'I have an idea that I will invent a new name for my books to supplant "novel". A new – by Virginia Woolf. But what? Elegy?' (Woolf 1982: 34). Woolf's idea for 'a new name' and its implied mingling of forms speaks to this study's two principal areas of enquiry. Her 'quarrel with grieving', as the title of Mark Spilka's study has it, her various attempts to write elegy-as-novel, and her struggles to deal with her mother's death typify the questions the elegist always has to answer: Can I grieve in writing? What is the best form for doing so? How do I balance writing about the deceased with the fact that writing grief makes me my own subject? At the same time, the possibility that a novel might be an elegy exemplifies the particular difficulties in giving an account of elegy written in the last hundred years or so. If a novel can be an elegy then we have already travelled some considerable distance from elegy as a sub-genre of poetry. And if a novel can be an elegy then so can almost any other cultural product; and if that is so then where does that leave poetic elegy? Finally, if a novel, the traditional picture of life, can be an elegy then this suggests that our experience of loss is not just confined to our responses to death. Loss may, in fact, be inextricable from our general experience.

Following the implications of Woolf's 'new name', then, elegy is as likely to be a distinctive idiom, mode of enquiry or species of self-description as a distinctive form. In terms of poetry, the distance between canonical and contemporary elegy and between sub-genre and idiom is highlighted by the title of John Ash's poem 'Elegy, Replica, Echo: in memoriam John Griggs 1941–91' (Ash 2002: 24). Ash's 27-line elegy comprises a desultory account of the funeral and oblique references to transmigration and talking with the dead and suggests that the closer we move to our own time, the harder it becomes to talk about elegy with any sense of distinctiveness beyond the word itself. Indeed, Ash's title might be said to portray the way modern funeral elegies are fainter and fainter copies of an unobtainable original. The critical difficulty in writing about elegy *and* the generality of loss is brilliantly caught in another Ash poem which says of the death of his mother that 'It felt strange, but sad and regrettable only in the sense/that everything is sad and regrettable, or potentially so' (Ash 2002: 79).

Elegy began as poetry and it is with poetry that any account of it must also begin. Ash's 'everything ... potentially so' connects with the way that elegy in English poetry has always been, in John Hollander's phrase, a mood rather than a formal mode (Hollander 1975: 200). Similarly, Dennis Kay has called elegy 'a form without frontiers' (Kay 1990: 7). Douglas Dunn's *Elegies* (1985), which gathers 39 poems commemorating his first wife Lesley who died from cancer in 1981, is a recent example of the importance of mood and diverse form. Some poems deal specifically with his wife's illness and death but most are autobiographical and describe the poet's progress through mourning towards a new life. The book includes sonnets, *terza rima*, blank and free verse and typifies elegy's remarkable hospitality to different styles and modes. Dunn's book can be said to combine two of elegy's principal meanings in English poetry: a song of lamentation, in particular a funeral song or lament for the dead; and, in addition, meditative or reflective verse, more properly termed elegiac poetry.

Elegy's shifting definitions have their roots in its classical origins. The word derives from the Greek *elegos* which, although it had some distant connotations of mourning, originally described a poem written in elegiac distich, a couplet composed of a hexameter followed by a pentameter. The subject matter of an *elegos* could be anything from politics to love and the Alexandrian Greeks used the form primarily for erotic verse and lovers' complaints. Among the Latin writers, Ovid continued this trend but started to extend the range of elegy's subjects. As we shall see in Chapter 2 'What was elegy?', elegy's other important derivation is the pastoral forms known as eclogues or idylls. Elegy's shepherds and its movement from grief to consolation have their origins in poems such as the 'Lament for Bion', Theocritus's 'First Idyll' and Virgil's Fifth and Tenth Eclogues.

Classical elegy's range of subject matter continued when the term started to be used in English poetry. Its first appearance, 'I tell mine elegie', is in Alexander Barclay's fifth *Eclogue* 'The Cytezen and Uplondyshman' (1514) in which two shepherds debate the familiar subject of town versus country life and relate a fable of the origin of society's different classes.[1] One of the first poems to be called an elegy by its author is George Gascoigne's 'The Complaint of Philomene' (1562). The word appears in the poem's dedication to Lord Wilton and Gascoigne's '*Elegye* or sorrowfull song' underlines the genre's classical origins by re-telling the myth of Philomela whom the gods turned into a swallow. Elegy's amatory and erotic connotations are also found throughout the sixteenth century. A sonnet from Michael Drayton's *Idea* beginning 'Yet read at last the story of my woe' offers the poet's beloved 'My life's complaint in dolefull elegies' (in Evans, ed., 2003: 101). Marlowe made frankly erotic translations of Ovid's *Elegia*. Similarly, John Donne's 'To his Mistress Going to Bed', written in the mid-1590s, was originally one of a group of untitled 'Elegies'. The generalized meaning of elegy continued to be used throughout the following centuries with an increasing emphasis on subjectivity and style. The eighteenth-century pastoral poet William Shenstone wrote a range of elegies with titles such as 'To a lady, on the language of birds' and 'He complains how soon the pleasing novelty of life is over'. He took permission from classical writers' range of subject matter and the fact that 'there have been few rules given us by critics concerning the structure of elegiac poetry'. He argued that elegy's 'peculiar characteristic' is

> a tender and querulous idea ... and so long as this is thoroughly sustained, admits of a variety of subjects; which by its manner of treating them, it renders its own. It throws its melancholy stole over pretty different objects; which, like the dresses at a funeral procession, gives them all a kind of solemn and uniform appearance.
>
> (Shenstone 1768: 15–16)

The idea of elegy as a manner continued into the Romantic period and beyond but with an important modification. Coleridge was able to remark that,

> Elegy is a form of poetry natural to the reflective mind. It *may* treat of any subject, but it must treat of no subject *for itself*; but always and exclusively with reference to the poet. As he will feel regret for the past or desire for the future, so sorrow and love become the principal themes of the elegy. Elegy presents every thing as lost and gone, or absent and future.
>
> (Coleridge 1835: 268, original emphasis)

The key phrase is 'exclusively with reference to the poet'. Coleridge is stressing the authority and authenticity of individual feeling.

Shenstone's simile of 'the dresses at a funeral procession' underlines how quickly elegy became strongly identified with a poetry of mourning. Funeral elegy as a distinctive genre also has its origins in the sixteenth century. Dennis Kay has argued convincingly that this was a direct consequence of the English Reformation. The disappearance of the Catholic Requiem Mass and the proscription of prayers for the repose of the dead shifted the emphasis of funeral observances not only towards the secular but also towards the living. The fate of the soul of the deceased gave way to the state of his or her survivors (Kay 1990: 2–3). As we shall see in Chapter 2, Edmund Spenser is particularly important in the establishment of funeral elegy as a distinctive sub-genre in this period. In the 'November' eclogue of *The Shepheardes Calender* (1579) and his pastoral elegy for Sir Philip Sidney, 'Astrophel' (1595), he begins to work with a range of figures and stylistic and structural patterns which later elegists would turn into characteristics of the genre. The use of recurring figures and patterns by poets such as Milton, Shelley, Tennyson, Arnold, Swinburne and Yeats emphasizes how funeral elegy, like elegiac poetry, is not a fixed form like a sonnet. Shenstone's simile of 'the dresses at a funeral procession' and Coleridge's emphasis on authenticity highlight how funeral elegy has depended, to borrow Shenstone's words and rework them, on the wearing or invocation of a solemn uniform. The elegist borrows this uniform from his predecessors to convince us of his seriousness and depth of feeling so that an elegy, more than any other genre of poetry, is a poem made out of other poems. When Milton refers to 'the oaten flute' in 'Lycidas' he echoes 'pipes of oaten reed' in Spenser's 'Astrophel'. Similarly, 'The soul of Adonais, like a star' at the climax of Shelley's poem echoes Milton's figuring of Lycidas as 'the day-star' that 'flames in the forehead of the morning sky'. Shelley's 'Life, like a dome of many-coloured glass' in 'Adonais' (LII) perhaps glimmers distantly behind the 'windowless dome' in John Ash's 'Elegy, Replica, Echo'.

Funeral elegy emerges with real distinctiveness at the beginning of the seventeenth century with the work of two poets, John Donne and John Milton. The connection between death and elegy is made clear by Donne's 'An Anatomy of the World: The First Anniversary' (1611) whose third section is entitled 'A Funeral Elegy'. Donne's lasting achievement, as Dennis Kay reminds us, was to create 'an innovatory non-pastoral funeral mode' by modifying Latin models and 'writing in an argumentative register appropriate to conversation, satire, and the dramatic expression of inner turmoil' (Kay 1990: 95). The argumentative register combined with direct vernacular can be heard throughout the nineteenth and twentieth centuries in elegies as superficially diverse as Tennyson's 'In Memoriam' (1850) and Auden's 'In Memory of W. B. Yeats' (1939). Milton's 'Lycidas' (1637/1645) revived and reworked the tropes of pastoral elegy into a well-defined progress from grief to consolation and detachment. This provided later elegists with a more attractive template than Donne's 'argumentative register' but Milton's influence can be traced in two other aspects of elegy. First, 'Lycidas' makes explicit pastoral elegy's function as a space of poetic initiation and succession. Second, its setting by the sea has become a recurrent trope visible, for example, in Hardy's elegy for Swinburne 'A Singer Asleep' (1910); in section IV of T. S. Eliot's 'The Waste Land', 'Death by Water' (1922); and in Elizabeth Bishop's memorial for Robert Lowell 'North Haven' (1978). The sea figures, in the words of Ariel's song from *The Tempest*, the possibility of 'a sea change' into a 'rich and strange' consolatory apotheosis. It is a possibility with which later elegists have sought both positive and negative feedbacks.

The preceding paragraphs might appear to suggest that while there has always been blurring of elegy and elegiac poetry, of mode and mood, funeral elegy was somehow 'settled' at some point in the past. Indeed, in his seminal study *The English Elegy: Studies in the Genre from Spenser to Yeats* (1985), Peter Sacks was able to detail recurring primary and secondary conventions. The primary conventions include: a pastoral context; the use of repetitions, refrains and repeated questions; outbursts of anger and cursing; a procession of mourners; a movement from grief to consolation; and concluding images of resurrection. The secondary conventions include: division of mourning between several voices; questions of reward, contest and inheritance between elegist and subject; the elegist's reluctant submission to language and an accompanying protestation of incapacity; and his need to draw attention to his own surviving powers (Sacks 1985: 2). However, Jahan Ramazani was unable to take a similar approach in his study of modern elegy from Hardy to Heaney. Modern elegists, he points out, have tended to attack convention and often leave their readers and themselves inconsolable (Ramazani 1994: 1–4). What tropes we might be able to identify, such as digging and burial in Thomas Hardy's 'Ah, are you digging on my grave?' (1914), Wilfred Owen's 'Miners' (1918) and Seamus Heaney's so-called 'bog poems' (1972–75), are distant and isolated. More to the point, as W. David Shaw observes, the elegist's traditional reticence and anxieties become 'open sites of fracture and breakdown' (Shaw 1994a: 147). Similarly, Celeste M. Schenck notes strong tendencies in modern elegy towards 'parody and inversion' and 'deliberate rupture of ceremonial patterns' which 'results in works that are generically mutant'. She borrows Abbie Findlay Potts's description of Shelley's *Alastor* (1816) to name such works *'élégies manquées'* (Schenck 1986b: 108). For Potts, an 'elegy manqué' offers no 'new light or new life' and often fails to get beyond 'a vague literary melancholia, an indistinct idyll of social failure' (Potts 1967: 244).

All these estimates offer telling insights into modern elegy but none takes into account the extent to which poetry itself and wider attitudes to experience have become overwhelmingly elegiac. The reasons for wider elegiac attitudes are complex but, from an English perspective, would certainly include what Blake Morrison identified in Philip Larkin's poetry as 'post imperial tristesse' (in Corcoran 1993: 87). One would also have to take account of the rise of the postwar heritage industry and its commodified nostalgia. In a wider sense, philosophers such as Slavoj Žižek and Giorgio Agamben have argued that we live in a profoundly melancholic age and that melancholy involves not only an attachment to loss but also the pleasurable anticipation of loss (Žižek 2000: 657–63). Attitudes to death and mourning have also undergone significant changes in the last 20 years or so. Where commentators such as Philippe Ariès (1981: 559–616) and Geoffrey Gorer (1965: passim) were able to write with some justification of the denial of death and mourning throughout much of the twentieth century this is no longer the case. Death and mourning have become participatory, public spectacles. Live television coverage of events such as 9/11, the Beslan school siege and the 2004 Asian tsunami and documentaries that seek to explore 'what happened next' have detached grief from personal loss. Anyone who lives in a city will have seen flowers placed at the sites of road accidents; and, since the end of the Second World War, national identity has become synonymous with remembrance.

The dominance of elegiac poetry also has interesting origins within poetry itself. Large areas of contemporary poetry seem, in Coleridge's terms, to '[present] every thing as lost and gone, or absent and future' to the extent that poetry often seems like a sub-genre of elegy as opposed to the other way round. This may at some level be symptomatic of poetry's fallen cultural status, a kind of self-mourning. However, two aspects of poetry are closely linked to contemporary poetry's overwhelmingly elegiac mood. First, as William Watkin has argued in a wide-ranging study of loss and commemoration in contemporary writing, all elegies 'have a lot to teach us about the non-representability of absence and the permanent trace of all this in all forms of representation' (Watkin 2004: 59). Second, contemporary poetry is dominated by the speaking 'I'. We have become so accustomed to this that we hardly notice it but a comparison of, say, Robin Skelton's *Poetry of the Thirties* (1964) with an anthology of British and Irish poetry of the 1980s and 1990s, *The New Poetry* (1993), reveals this as a distinctly contemporary phenomenon. The dominance of the speaking 'I' converges with the elegiac because, as Adrian Kear argues in a study of the public mourning of Princess Diana, identity is itself 'a melancholic structure in that, in order to maintain subjective consistency and illusory integrity, the ego has to repudiate or foreclose those identifications that enabled it to come into being' (in Kear and Steinberg, eds, 1999: 183). The self develops and asserts itself by holding loss within itself.

In the following chapters, I do not attempt to offer a comprehensive survey of elegy. Instead I discuss a range of elegies from the canonical to the contemporary in order to explore established and emergent reading practices. Chapter 2 'What was elegy?' outlines the classical Greek origins of elegy, the entry of the genre into English literature and the characteristics of the genre. Chapter 3 'The work of mourning' surveys the psychoanalytic ideas that underlie criticism of elegy. Chapter 4 'The needs of ghosts' focuses on the modern elegy's scepticism about and rejection of transcendence and consolation, exploring how AIDS and breast-cancer elegies typify this anti-elegiac turn. Chapter 5 'Female elegists and feminist readers' surveys female elegy, feminist scholarship and work by female psychoanalysts which challenges dominant Freudian models of the work of mourning. Chapter 6 'After mourning: virtual bodies, aporias and the work of dread' explores other challenges to established thinking about death and elegy that have come recently from cultural studies, philosophy and literary criticism. Finally, Chapter 7 'Elegy diffused, elegy revived' addresses the diffusion of the elegiac mode in contemporary poetry; the diffusion of elegy beyond poetry; the changed nature of the relation between public and private; and the revival of elegy as a distinct consolatory form by a small number of contemporary poets.

2

WHAT WAS ELEGY?

Chris O'Connell's play *Hymns* (1999) portrays four young men reuniting to mourn the loss of a close male friend who has committed suicide. Their struggle to come to terms with their grief results in an unstable mixture of jokes, arguments, reminiscences and confessions. The dialogue is interspersed with passages of intense physical theatre. In one physical sequence from Frantic Assembly's 2005 production, the four men leap around and over a table, taking it in turns to lie on it like a corpse. The play climaxes with the smashing of the urn containing the friend's ashes. This is followed by a question 'Why do men die before women?' which is answered 'Because they want to' (O'Connell 2005: 57). The play ends with more jokes as three of the men climb a ladder into the darkness above the stage in what looks like a literal attempt to rise above the trauma of loss.

Hymns is not, of course, an elegy. Nonetheless, the play can be said to stage the characteristic scene of many elegies: men mourning the untimely deaths of other men. Similarly, although the subjects of elegies are not usually suicides, the play's closing question and answer converge with the way the genre often dramatizes the possibility that an untimely death may have been chosen or invited. In Theocritus's 'First Idyll', written in the third century BC, Daphnis deliberately chooses not to live. In the nineteenth century, 'Thyrsis', Matthew Arnold's elegy for his friend Arthur Hugh Clough, suggests that Clough's death is connected to the fact that 'his piping took a troubled sound/Of storms that rage outside our happy ground' (Arnold 1959: 221). A final interesting convergence between *Hymns* and elegy comes in a short exchange just before the urn is shattered: 'Be careful with it.' 'Yeah ... Don't want to lose him twice, do we?' (O'Connell 2005: 56). As we shall see, elegists have been concerned that the writing out of loss does not distance the deceased even further but turns loss into something of use for the survivors.

Elegy, like *Hymns*, journeys to the limits of understanding and asks how it is possible to live with death. The origins and characteristics of elegy are the subject of the remainder of this chapter. The past tense of the title 'What was elegy?' serves two functions. It underlines that much of the chapter is concerned with literary history. Crucially, it speaks to the fact that elegy's conventions no longer seem as settled as they once did. Indeed, as W. David Shaw has observed, 'the most authoritative critical histories' of the genre 'are encoded ... in the elegy's own testing of conventions'; and good readers are as much involved in this testing as great elegists (Shaw 1994b: 1, 16).

THE ORIGINS OF ELEGY

The origins of elegy involve poetic form and subject matter. The word elegy derives, dictionaries tell us, from the Greek *elegos* meaning 'mournful song' but the earliest surviving examples are not funereal. Elegies written in Greece in the seventh century BC by poets such as Archilochus, Callinus and Tyrtaeus dealt with war and love, offered philosophical advice or sent good wishes to travelling friends. These poems came to be known as elegies because they were written in elegiac couplets which alternate dactylic hexameters and pentameters. They were traditionally accompanied by the flute or the oboe-like, two-piped *aulos*. As Martin L. West observes, elegy merely denotes a large body of verse in which the poet spoke in his own person, often to a specific addressee, and in the context of a particular event or state of affairs. West argues that the sheer diversity of subject matter makes it unlikely the poems were originally called elegies because the ancient Greeks named forms according to the occasions for which they were written, for example paean or hymenaeus. The earliest elegies had no name because they had no single function (West 1974: 2, 7).

The diversity of early elegy does not mean that it was never funereal. Margaret Alexiou thinks it likely that there was a sixth-century BC school of Dorian elegists who used the elegiac couplet for lament (Alexiou 1974: 104). We can also point to the collection of elegies *Lyde* by Antimachus who flourished around 400 BC. It was named after the poet's mistress and in it he attempted to find consolation for her death by working through a series of exempla derived from mythological stories of unhappy love affairs. The Greek poems that have had the greatest influence on funeral elegy are those by the third-century BC poets Theocritus, Bion and Moschus. Theocritus (c. 303–c. 240 BC), generally acknowledged as the creator of pastoral poetry, wrote a series of 'eidullia', literally 'little poems' but commonly called idylls. These idylls, also known as eclogues, establish not only a range of characters and imagery such as nymphs and shepherds or singing and weaving but also the close relation between pastoral and elegy, hence the term pastoral elegy.

Theocritus's 'First Idyll' begins with Thyrsis, a shepherd, meeting a goatherd at noon. They praise each other's piping and the goatherd persuades Thyrsis to sing 'The Affliction of Daphnis' for the prize of an elaborately decorated cup. The ballad Thyrsis sings describes how Daphnis, the ideal shepherd, pines away for love, refusing to speak. It is in three parts: a complaint to the Nymphs for allowing Daphnis to get into this state and a gathering of herdsmen and others around the silent, dying man; the appearance of the Love-Goddess who upbraids Daphnis and persuades him to break his silence; and Daphnis's dying speech in which he bequeaths his pipe to Pan and addresses all nature. Theocritus' poem is notable because it establishes a number of conventions and figures that become characteristics of funeral elegy in English. These include: the invocation of a muse; the rebuking of nymphs for not being present to prevent death; a procession of mourners, in this case animals, shepherds and divine beings; the use of pathetic fallacy, that is the attribution of human emotions to the world of nature; a sense of the natural order being disrupted by death; catalogues of flowers and animals; and the apotheosis of the dead person.

Thyrsis, a shepherd-poet, sings of the death of another shepherd-poet Daphnis, a portrayal that is reworked in, for example, Milton's 'Lycidas' and Arnold's 'Thyrsis'. The opening of Theocritus's poem also portrays funeral elegy as a competitive genre. The unnamed goatherd promises Thyrsis the prize of the cup if he can sing 'The Affliction of Daphnis' as well as he did in a recent contest with Chromis of Libya. Elegies, then, are forms that are repeated and repeatable. More to the point, the placing of 'The Affliction of Daphnis' in the context of a contest underlines elegy as a self-conscious performance in which the elegist asserts his own poetic skill and becomes part of a pre-existent tradition or lineage of similarly skilled poets. As we shall see later in this chapter, contests and inheritance are recurring figures in English elegy.

'The Affliction of Daphnis' also introduces the connections between mourning and nature which later elegists repeat. Thyrsis tells us that 'when Daphnis died the foxes wailed' and the cattle moaned for him (ll. 71–75). At the end of the poem Daphnis addresses nature directly: 'Bear violets now ye briers, ye thistles violets too;/Daffodil may hang on the juniper, and all things go askew' (ll. 132–33). Most importantly, Theocritus's 'First Idyll' establishes the relationship between speech and silence to which later elegists habitually return. For the first third of the poem Daphnis is silent: 'But never a word said the poor neatherd, for a bitter love bare he' (ll. 92–93). He is finally provoked into speaking by the Goddess of Love and tells his listeners of his impending silence and absence. The emphasis on silence and absence converges with the way in which later elegists have explored the elegy as a structure for mourning and consolation that is always on the verge of breaking down and whose efficacy is therefore perpetually in doubt. Thyrsis's song begins by asking 'Where were ye, Nymphs . . . ?' and Daphnis's own speech makes plain the hopelessness of his situation. Even the Goddess cannot save him: there is no help to be had. As we shall see, later ele-

gists return time and again to this sense of belatedness. Thyrsis
makes a poem out of Daphnis abandoning poetry which highlights how, in William Watkin's words, 'the problems of elegy
remain those of language itself ... Elegy consists of making
physical, material works of art out of the very event that destroys
our own physicality' (Watkin 2004: 6).

Peter Sacks draws attention to the 'division between or within
mourning voices' in elegy and this is also present in Theocritus's
poem (Sacks 1985: 34). Thyrsis sings 'The Affliction of Daphnis'
but within the poem Daphnis's death is mourned in turn by
Hermes, Priapus, the Goddess of Love and Daphnis himself.
Different mourning voices are also present in two other third-
century BC poems, Bion's 'Lament for Adonis' and Moschus's
'Lament for Bion' which Shelley drew on for 'Adonais'. In Bion's
poem, Adonis is mourned by Aphrodite, Echo, The Graces and
The Wedding God; and in Moschus's poem mourning is divided
between nature, cities and mythological figures. Both poems,
like Theocritus's 'First Idyll', feature repeated refrains. Moschus's
lament is particularly notable for leaving no analogy unexplored
in expressing the enormity of grief – not even Homer, Pindar
and Theocritus were mourned as much – and for ending with the
poet downplaying his own powers: 'If I had such power with
the pipe as Bion with harp, I would myself sing before Pluteus.'

The third-century elegists established two other important
characteristics. First, in contrast to the usual dialogue of pastoral
poetry, they made the elegy into a monody, that is a poem voiced
by a single speaker. Milton and Arnold subtitled 'Lycidas' and
'Thyrsis' with the term. Second, neither the poets nor the members
of their audience were goatherds or shepherds: they would have been
citizens of city states. The setting of Theocritus's poem highlights
how elegy locates mourning outside the usual routines and
habitual interactions of the individual and the wider community.

ELEGY IN ENGLISH: CHAUCER TO SPENSER

The third-century Greek elegists established a set of conventions
and a bank of imagery that recur in English elegies from Spenser
to Auden. It would be wrong, however, to assume that conventions

and imagery simply arrived when the Renaissance reached England and seeded a whole new genre. Personal elegy starts to appear at the end of the Middle Ages and comes in five main types: laments for monarchs, poems about the fall of the mighty, political poems, warnings from the dead and allegorical dream visions. One particularly interesting example of the last type is Chaucer's *The Book of the Duchess* which, although not influential on later elegies, illuminates the literary portrayal of mourning. The poem was written c. 1370 and is believed to have been composed in honour of Blanche, Duchess of Lancaster, who died in 1368. It begins with the poet reading a fictional account of grief, the story of Ceyx and Alcyone from Ovid's *Metamorphoses* Book XI, which focuses on Alcyone's mourning for her drowned husband. Having finished the book, the poet falls asleep and dreams first of a hunt and then of finding a knight 'clothed al in blake' in a wood (l. 457). The knight is grieving for the death of his lady. The rest of the poem describes his grief and her virtues. The poem ends with the poet waking up and resolving that he 'wol, be processe of time,/Fonde to put this swevene in ryme' (ll. 1331–32) ('will, in process of time/attempt to write this dream in rhyme').

The Book of the Duchess has many convergences with later elegies. As Helen Philips points out, it has elements of praise and mourning, explores loss from a number of perspectives and uses a pre-existent genre to elevate its subject (Philips and Harvey, eds, 1997: 29–30). *The Book of the Duchess* begins with reading and ends with writing. Death and mourning are too painful to be confronted directly and can only be approached through the words of others, through pre-existent stories. In our own time, Douglas Dunn's *Elegies* begins with a poem entitled 'Re-reading Katherine Mansfield's *Bliss and Other Stories*' and ends with the poet looking forward to returning to his 'desk of rhymes' (Dunn 1985: 9, 64). The story of our grief must always be someone else's first before it can be ours. The use of pre-existent stories and others' griefs highlights elegy as a self-conscious literary performance. *The Book of the Duchess* moves through reading, dreaming, the hunt and the knight's story itself to arrive at a core of terrible loss. The use of an embedded narrative is present in Theocritus but in Chaucer's poem it is notable as a way of dealing with the pain of loss, with transience and mutability. The sense of a narrative journey to grief and back is an important characteristic of elegy; and the multi-faceted elegy is visible in works as superficially diverse as John Donne's 'An Anatomy of the World: The First Anniversary' and W. H. Auden's 'In Memory of W. B. Yeats'. Finally, Chaucer's poem not only fails to offer explicit consolation but remains ambivalent about the efficacy of literature. The knight rejects the narrator's many offers of comfort: 'No man may my sorwe glade' (l. 563). Similarly, the poem's own artfulness, such as its figuring of Fortune as a wily chess player and its moving portrayal of the Duchess, ultimately fails as consolation.

The other principal types of medieval elegy survived into the early modern period. Tudor poets such as Barnabe Googe, George Turbeville and George Whetstone, and, indeed, many of their seventeenth-century successors, either wrote in generalities or made poems that were essentially compilations of the acts and qualities of dead celebrities. The elegies and epitaphs gathered in *The Penguin Book of Renaissance Verse 1509–1659* reveal a double emphasis on the physical facts of burial and bodily decay. Poem after poem portrays the 'urne', 'Tombe' or 'Marble Hearse' in which a public figure or loved one turns to 'dust'. Thomas Churchyard (c. 1520–1604) was one of the most prolific elegists of the period. Spenser had Colin Clout say of him that he 'sung so long until quite hoarse he grew'. He was primarily a public poet and titles like 'A sad and solemne funeral of the right honourable Sir Frances Knowles' and 'Sad and heavy verses . . . for the losse of the Archbishop of Canterbury' are typical of his output. Churchyard was certainly no innovator and even his contemporaries thought his style heavy and old-fashioned. Dennis Kay notes that nearly all his elegies imagined their subjects finding celestial happiness in Abraham's bosom (Kay 1990: 19). Churchyard exemplifies the fact that the elegies that posterity has deemed original have been the exception and not the rule.

A few poets did distinguish themselves from the standard operating procedures that Churchyard represents. Nicholas Grimald (c. 1519–c. 1562) combined highly personal material with artistic self-consciousness in ways that prefigure many aspects of the later English elegy. 'A funeral song, upon the deceas of Annes his mother' mixes homely, intimate detail with learned allusions:

> Now linen clothes, wrought with those fingers fine,
> Now other thynges of yours dyd you make mine:
> Tyll your last thredes gan Clotho to untwyne,
> And of your dayes the date extreme assygne.
> (In Norbrook and Woudhuysen, eds, 1993: 630)

The repeated rhyme, coming in a lengthy passage of couplets, gives a sense of the verse itself starting to 'untwyne' and is typical of the innovations Grimald brought to elegy. We might also note his use of the figure of weaving which, as Peter Sacks has noted, recurs throughout the genre (Sacks 1985: 18). But the most striking aspect of Grimald's poetry is its directness: there is a rawness that seems more of our own time than the poet's.

The self-conscious art that distinguishes Grimald's elegies, or Surrey's 'Wyatt resteth here' with its 38 lines for the poet's age, becomes a key characteristic of elegy in the work of Edmund Spenser (c. 1552–99). It is with Spenser that the close identification of the elegy and pastoral in English poetry begins. Dennis Kay observes that Renaissance writers viewed the pastoral as 'hospitable to many genres' and 'a vehicle for literary experiment' (Kay 1990: 29). More to the point, as we saw in our earlier discussion of Theocritus, pastoral was already closely identified with elegy. The pastoral narrative, in which workers leave their labours to engage in debate or poetic competition and then return to work, allowed a crucial double emphasis. The pastoral becomes a kind of retreat, a turning aside from everyday concerns and routines, a clearing of imaginative and poetic space in which to contemplate fundamentals. At the same time, the pastoral is at once a place of work and an interlude from work and this suggests that its imaginative and poetic work is inextricable from those everyday concerns and routines. It is almost as if the imaginative work of pastoral must be completed so that more prosaic work can continue. Pastoral elegy, then, examines change and loss against continuity.

The 'November' eclogue of Spenser's *The Shepheardes Calendar* (1579) is the first pastoral elegy in English. It begins with a conversation between two shepherd-poets, Thenot and Colin Clout. Thenot asks Colin to perform 'songs of some iouisaunce' but Colin replies that the time of year 'sadder plight doth aske'. Thenot then proposes a more appropriate subject: 'For dead is Dido, dead alas and drent,/Dido the great shephearde his daughter sheene'. In return for the poem, Thenot will give Colin a lamb and other gifts if it is as good as his usual love poetry. Colin's song is a response to a commission and this highlights that an elegist does not have to have a close relationship with his subject in order to mourn. Another important aspect of Spenser's poem is its announcement of its own originality. Thomas Churchyard had written that he was 'not striving to shewe any rare invention' (in Kay 1990: 18). The originality of *The Shepheardes Calendar* is made explicit in the poem's dedicatory epistle to Spenser's friend Gabriel Harvey by one 'E. K.'. E. K. makes clear that Spenser is doing something new in English poetry, something very different from 'the rakehylle route of our ragged rymers'. He is clearly a better poet but one reason for this is his awareness of tradition, starting with Theocritus. However, Spenser will not make clumsy imitations of past masters but use that tradition as a spur to 'keepe wing with the best'. Elegy is therefore identified as the form where the poet demonstrates his skill and where only a part of that skill derives from his reworking of earlier poems. In this context, E. K. functions as Spenser's paratextual persona: he stands outside the poem not only pointing out through 'glosses' where Spenser conforms with or departs from tradition but also indicating the nature of elegy as palimpsest.

'November' is in 15 ten-line stanzas and the first of these tells us much about the originality Spenser was aiming for:

> Vp then *Melpomene* thou mournefulst Muse of nyne,
> Such cause of mourning neuer hadst afore:
> Vp grieslie ghosts and vp my rufull ryme,
> Matter of myrth now shalt thou haue no more.
> For dead shee is, that myrth thee made of yore.

Dido my deare alas is dead,
Dead and lyeth wrapt in lead:
O heauie herse,
Let streaming tears be poured out in store:
O carefull verse.
                              (Spenser 1965: 461)

Spenser combines a learned allusion to Melpomene with everyday speech in lines that are as plainly moving as they are carefully worked. The invocation of Melpomene is not just a convention: it signals an entry into the public spaces of literature and history. The form of the stanza itself is particularly noteworthy. The first line is an alexandrine which is followed by four decasyllabic lines, two tetrameters, a dimeter, another decasyllabic line and a final dimeter. This gives the effect of recurrent waves of emotion. The first line is a full outpouring of feeling that gradually subsides through shorter and shorter lines, until in the penultimate line it reappears in one last outburst. The poem itself is divided into 11 stanzas of mourning and four of consolation. The division is underlined by the refrain changing from 'O heauie herse ... O carefull verse' to 'O happy herse ... O joyfull verse'. Thenot's reception of the poem also signals its complexity: 'O francke shepheard, how bene thy verses meint/ With doolful pleasaunce, so as I ne wotte/Whether rejoice or weepe for great constrainte?' Thenot originally requested 'songs of some iouisaunce' and has received some after all. Elegy, then, is not just consolation but a means of making death somehow acceptable. Thenot is responding as much to the art of Colin's poem as to its subject.

The art of the poem is not just in the service of making consolation palatable for its listener. Its complex stanza form can be said to perform both the emotional work of mourning and address some of the paradoxes involved in elegy. The first 11 stanzas explore grief in order to exhaust it so that consolation may begin. Colin Clout's penultimate line is 'My woe now wasted is'. At the same time, they ask but do not answer the question of how absence is to be represented and made acceptable. Dido is someone of whom 'nought remaynes but the memoree' and who is now a 'soule unbodied'. 'Perform' is, then, a particularly apt word because, as W. David Shaw has noted, elegies are acts of performative language. They cannot afford to be merely descriptive: they have to do what they say and almost make things happen (Shaw 1994b: 13). Elegies cannot just describe loss: they have to refigure it as a species of transformation and provide an early glimpse of an afterlife for their subject. We can find this in Theocritus's 'First Idyll' where Daphnis portrays himself among the dead blaming the Goddess of Love for his fate. Spenser addresses Dido directly: 'I see thee blessed soule, I see,/Walke in *Elisian* fields so free'. No one, of course, knows what a 'soule' looks like so the poet then reverts to conventional descriptions of Elysium. However, Dido is pictured 'with the blessed Gods in blisse,/There drincks she *Nectar* with *Ambrosia* mixt'. It is a drink which, as E. K.'s 'glosse' makes clear, combines pagan and Christian elements.

Spenser's 'November' eclogue establishes a number of important aspects of pastoral elegy in English poetry. An elegy that wants to rise above the output of 'ragged rymers' must fashion itself out of the best recognizable precedents. E. K.'s 'glosse' refers to Plato, Virgil, Lydgate, Chaucer and George Gascoigne's 'The Complaint of Philomene'. This 'rising above' is an important part of the elegiac performance. The transformation of the deceased subject is the occasion for the poet's art to undergo a similar transformation. 'November' also shows the negotiations and adaptations that take place between classical precedents and Christian belief. Most importantly, the poem shows that the elegist cannot avoid grappling with the unrepresentability of absence. A death prompts the narration of a life. The particularities of that life become crucial in the face of the anonymity of death.

ELEGY IN ENGLISH: FIGURING LOSS

Dennis Kay argues that for 'any elegy with artistic pretension' Spenser's 'November' eclogue 'established as a central principle the necessary conjunction of praise, invention, and participation in a vital tradition' (Kay 1990: 37). We can add that the poem also established another necessary conjunction of English elegy: the reinterpretation of convention and a broad scepticism about how to figure and represent loss. 'Figure' is a key word because it combines senses of representation, of making estimates and of working out in order to achieve understanding. It is not my intention to work through how successive elegists have used the characteristics we noted in our discussion of Theocritus. Such a survey has already been brilliantly done by Peter Sacks. Taking my lead from Sacks's discussion of Spenser, I shall instead focus on the figuration of loss and how scepticism about figuration has itself become a characteristic elegiac figure.

The elegist starts from a negative position. Positives, made into negatives by death, must somehow be made into positives again or have that transformation compensated for. His love or, perhaps more properly, his desire for the deceased, must be narrated as loss, as dispossession. Allen Ginsberg coins the word 'lacklove' for this in his elegy for his mother 'Kaddish' (Ginsberg 1987: 210). Kaddish is the ancient Jewish prayer that a mourner recites daily at public services for 11 months after the death of a parent or close relative and on subsequent anniversaries of the death. 'Lacklove' is a state whose persistence and emphasis on absence is overwhelming. We might note here how well 'lacklove' describes the condition of Daphnis in Theocritus's 'First Idyll' who seems determined to resist the power of love: 'But never word said the poor cowherd, for a bitter love bore he, and bore it to the end that was to be.' The persistence of loss is also stated clearly in Shelley's 'Adonais': 'grief returns with the revolving year' (XVIII). If only, he goes on, 'grief itself [were] mortal' but instead 'year [must] wake year to sorrow' (XXI). 'Rugby Chapel', Matthew Arnold's elegy for his father Thomas Arnold, figures the father as a 'mighty oak', now gone, who once gave shade. Now, 'For fifteen years,/We [...] have endured/Sunshine and rain as we might,/Bare, unshaded, alone' (Arnold 1959: 238).

The endurance of the unendurable is also behind the 'Question me again' that closes Seamus Heaney's 'Casualty' (Heaney 1979: 24). Heaney's poem belongs to a group of elegies in his collection *Field Work* that underline how elegists are always faced with unsatisfactory resurrections, unfinished and unfinishable conversations. The grief-as-exposure that we saw in Matthew Arnold is present in the way that several of Heaney's poems end out of doors in the chill of dawn or in an open boat. Imagery of drink and bread in several of Heaney's poems also underlines that elegy is only a temporary transubstantiation. Elegy, which appears to be and has often been treated critically as monumental, is in fact made occasional. Three of Heaney's elegies, 'A Postcard from North Antrim', 'Casualty' and 'In Memoriam Sean O'Riada', emphasize this further by resurrecting their subjects in repeatable situations: a party, a fishing trip and a concert (Heaney 1979: 19–20, 21, 29–30). The end of the poem is not the end of mourning: it only pretends to be, perhaps has to pretend to be. In the context of the Northern Irish Troubles, the language of several of Heaney's poems works to make their murdered subjects representative. As W. H. Auden wrote at the start of the Second World War in the opening lines of 'In Memory of Sigmund Freud', 'When there are so many we shall have to mourn,/Of whom shall we speak?' (Auden 1979: 91).

To return to Heaney briefly, several of his elegies feature images of the sea. The force of these is generally redemptive but more interesting is the figuring of the sea in 'Elegy' for the American poet Robert Lowell. Here the subject mocks Heaney's own 'fear of water' and is portrayed as a 'night ferry' crossing a 'big sea' that is 'ungovernable and dangerous' (Heaney 1979: 31–32). There is perhaps a distant nod to the 'perilous flood' and 'whelming tide' of Milton's 'Lycidas' but Heaney's imagery highlights how the elegist's writing out of negative love – 'lacklove' – is habitually accompanied by doubts about his own fitness for the task and his fear of falling short of his subject. Lowell is, of course, 'like' a night ferry because he has made the journey into death before the elegist and his other survivors. The elegist's voicing of his own inabilities also lies behind Tennyson's portrayal of himself in 'In Memoriam' as 'An infant crying in the night:/And with no language but a cry' (LIII). Later in the poem, Tennyson confesses that,

> I cannot love thee as I ought,
> For love reflects the thing beloved;
> My words are only words, and moved
> Upon the topmost froth of thought.
>
> (LI, ll. 1–4)

The passage exemplifies how scepticism about figuration becomes a figure. Words that can be carried upon the 'topmost forth' are inconsequential flotsam. Words can express love but love is here portrayed as a virtual space where the beloved only appears to be. Words and image are insubstantial in comparison with the previous corporeal existence of the deceased. Similarly, John Donne, mourning Elizabeth Drury some 200 years earlier, wrote of 'rags of paper', 'carcase verses, whose soul is not she', and asked 'can she [...] dwell in an elegy?'

The elegist protests his inability and, like Thomas Carew, mourning John Donne in 1633, asks forgiveness for his 'untun'd verse' and his 'panting numbers [...]/Gasping short winded Accents'. He may, like Carew, invoke a 'widdowed Poetry', but always manages, also like Carew, to 'breake [...]/The reverend silence that attends thy herse' (in Norbrook and Woudhuysen, eds, 1993: 743). Powerlessness, impotence and inactivity are transformed through the act of writing into power, potency and productivity. As Kate Lilley suggests, 'The crucial ambivalence of the elegy is that its narrative of loss may be rewritten as profit at strategic points [...] unsatisfied hunger redescribed as the return of appetite' (Lilley 1988: 50). Similarly, the loss that prompts the elegy becomes in the writing of the elegy a species of expenditure. In Lilley's words, 'the elegist spends himself in the service of desire, and the articulation of desire' and does so in an 'elegiac currency' of 'words, tears, sighs' (Lilley 1988: 51). One might add that many elegists seem to do so carelessly. One of the most extravagant examples of such expenditure is Shelley's 'Adonais' with its compulsive returns to tears and weeping. The repetitions of elegy such as the recurrence of the word 'gone' throughout Matthew Arnold's 'Thyrsis' are another example of expenditure.

The monetary imagery identified by Lilley is also explicit at the beginning of Tennyson's 'In Memoriam':

> I held it truth [...]
> [...]
> That men may rise on stepping-stones
> Of their dead selves to higher things.

> But who shall so *forecast* the years
> And find in *loss* a *gain* to match?
> Or reach a hand through time to catch
> The far-off *interest* of tears?
> (I, ll. 1–8, emphasis added)

Tennyson's questions voice a two-fold fear of expenditure. The self develops by spending itself but how, the poet asks, is such a gain to be guaranteed? In the same way, if mourning involves even greater self-expenditure how, the elegist asks, will I afford it? The poet's habitual anxiety about his skills is figured as a failure in financial forecasting. We will discuss the psychological workings of mourning in detail in Chapter 3, but it is worth noting here that monetary images of loss and expenditure appear in Freud's highly influential account of his grandson's game of 'fort/da' [gone/there]. Whenever the boy's mother left the room he would not cry but amuse himself by continually throwing away and retrieving toys, in particular a wooden reel with a piece of string tied round it. The interpretation of the game, Freud argues, is that the child '*compensated* himself' (emphasis added) for having allowed his mother to go away. Significantly, Freud introduces his observations by arguing that existing theories of children's play 'fail to bring into the foreground the *economic* motive, the consideration of the yield of pleasure involved' (Freud 1920/1984: 285, 283).

A literal monetary answer to Tennyson's 'who?' is, of course, the elegist. We might remember that Theocritus's Thyrsis and Spenser's Colin Clout both sang for a promised reward. Nonetheless, as we have seen, behind Tennyson's questions there is an anxiety about the poet's own coherence and survival. 'Dead selves' perhaps suggests an inherent instability which the work of mourning and the task of elegy will render even more precarious. In this context, the task of elegy, the poem that habitually begins in silence or confusion, is to produce the elegist's own coherent self. A few examples are instructive here. Milton's 'Lycidas' begins with its speaker 'the uncouth swain' arriving with 'forced fingers rude' to 'shatter' laurels, myrtles and ivy, which are themselves the ancient emblems of poetic power (Milton

1990: 39). It is an image of both the inert uselessness of poetic convention and the impossibility of the elegist's desire for his departed subject. The poem ends, in contrast, with images of poetic achievement, tranquillity and continuance:

> He touched the tender stops of various quills,
> With eager thought warbling his Doric lay:
> [...]
> At last he rose, and twitch'd his mantle blue:
> Tomorrow to fresh woods, and pastures new.
> (Milton 1990: 44)

The quicker rhythm of the second line suggests the onrush of new energy. Similarly, the coda of 'Lycidas' is in *ottava rima*, the intricate stanza of Italian epic. The performance of elegy has not only healed the elegist: it has revitalized him and raised his art to new heights of sophistication.

The movement from incoherence to coherent self is also found in elegies where the movement is less obvious than in 'Lycidas'. W. B. Yeats's 'In Memory of Major Robert Gregory' starts with an intention to 'name friends that cannot sup with us ... tonight being dead'. It ends by saying that although the poet had wanted to remember and, by implication, celebrate 'manhood', 'childhood' and 'boyish intellect', 'a thought/Of that late death took all my heart for speech' (Yeats 2000: 86–88). At first sight, this seems very odd: a lapsing into silence and a farewell to desire after 72 lines of poetry. However, as Peter Sacks points out 'all my heart for speech' also tells us that the poet has poured the entirety of himself into the poem (Sacks 1985: 297–98). The poem, its 'speech', becomes an emblem of the poet's survival and possibly of his own immortality. W. H. Auden's elegy for Yeats starts with an image of 'mercury [sinking] in the mouth of the dying day' but ends with a kind of uplifting prayer: 'In the prison of his days/Teach the free man how to praise' (Auden 1979: 83). This is Auden's lesson not Yeats's. The fact that he can draw it from the dead poet's work exemplifies the elegy's success and Auden's own creative powers. Finally, something similar can be observed in a very recent elegy, Andrew Bailey's 'Lodestar, Polestar' in memory of the poet Peter Redgrove (Bailey 2005: 38). Bailey's poem starts with a flooded village at night which is perhaps an oblique update of Milton's 'watery bier' (Milton 1990: 39). It then moves through a kind of celebration of Redgrove's poetic of visionary materialism, and ends with an image of stars rotating round a single star. Bailey's star echoes the ending of Milton's 'Lycidas' and the soul of the deceased figured as a star at the end of Shelley's 'Adonais'. But here it also seems to work as an image of Redgrove's poems, characterized by Neil Corcoran as 'wildly proliferating a dissipating and centrifugal imagery' (Corcoran 1993: 145).

Andrew Bailey's night-time journey from flooded village to new constellation converges with another important characteristic of elegy: that it occurs in a place and at a time divorced from everyday reality. These places and times are often simultaneously conceptual and literal. We have already noted how elegy's origins in pastoral mean it often utilizes images of retreat, of standing aside from daily routines and the wider community. Yeats's 'ancient tower' in 'In Memory of Major Robert Gregory'; Arnold's 'upland dim' in 'Thyrsis' which echoes while reversing 'the sun upon the Upland Lawn' in Gray's 'Elegy'; the 'neglected Spot' of Gray's poem; and Heaney sleepless at two a.m. in his 'Elegy' for Robert Lowell are all examples. Many elegies, like Gray's, are set at night or at the coming of night. The opening of Gray's poem depicts the progressive fading of external reality that 'leaves the world to darkness, and to me'. Elegies take place at night because of night's association with melancholy, and because night, such as Heaney's two a.m., is often the time of sleepless grief. The scene of night, whether explicitly figured so or not, also stands in for the dimness and incoherence with which many elegies begin. It is surely no coincidence that so many elegies place darkness, light and speech in a similar relation to that found at the beginning of Genesis. The elegist sets out to counter and resist chaos and oblivion. However, to return to Gray's 'Elegy', that 'to me' is crucial in the time and space of elegy. Like Daphnis in Theocritus's 'First Idyll' the elegist starts by seeking and asserting solitude. Partly this is self-protection: if one of the tasks of elegy is the production of a newly coherent and revitalized self, then the elegist needs no distractions. Similarly, Theocritus's anonymous goatherd reminds Thyrsis that, since Pan rests at midday, shepherds can't use their pipes for fear of disturbing him. The elegist must produce his voice without relying on any of his usual poetic props.

Matthew Arnold begins 'Thyrsis' surrounded by confusing change and feeling 'some loss of habit's power'; and even in the last lines of the poem Thyrsis's voice is a 'whisper' that has to compete with 'city noise' and 'the great town's harsh, heart-wearying roar' (Arnold 1959: 220, 224). The effort required to hear this whisper, the effort of producing the poem, should alert us to the fact that the elegist's solitude is necessarily a kind of self-regarding alienation. The elegist, ever watchful of himself, must move out of the world in order to move into the space of elegy. Even for a pastoral elegy it may seem incongruous that Arnold evokes a world of shepherds, pipes and swains in the mid-nineteenth century. To do so, however, conjures the beginnings of poetry itself and a consequent place of safety. The elegy, like the elm in Theocritus's 'First Idyll', is a place to sit out of the noonday glare. It is, of course, no accident that Arnold's poem tells how he and Thyrsis 'prized' a 'single elm-tree bright'. Arnold's elm looks back to Theocritus and to Gray's 'fav'rite Tree' just as Gray's closing evocation of 'Lawn' and 'Wood' looks back to the 'high lawns' and 'woods' at the beginning of Milton's 'Lycidas'. By creating a space apart and by often creating that space from previous elegiac spaces, the elegist signals that he is writing a different type of poem. The special space of elegy also figures the fact that graves are physically set apart from society; that bodies of mourned subjects are often lost; and that deaths often occur away from home.

Anxieties about the performance of masculinity may also lie behind the male elegist's turning aside. First, the night scene of elegy perhaps offers literal cover for the expression of love and desire for another man that may in other contexts be shameful. To borrow the words of the William Shenstone passage in the previous chapter, night itself functions as a 'melancholy stole ... like the dresses at a funeral procession', which gives the elegist's love for his subject an appropriately 'solemn appearance'. Second, lamentation risks charges of unmanliness. George Puttenham wrote in *The Arte of English Poesie* (1589) that

> to weepe for any sorrow ... is not so decent in a man: and therefore all high minded persons, when they cannot chuse but shed teares, wil turne away their face as a countenance undecent for a man to shew, and so will standers by till they have supprest such passion, thinking it nothing decent to behold such an uncomely countenance.
>
> (Puttenham 1589/1909: 296–97)

Women, in contrast, 'weepe and shed teares at every little greefe ... for by the common proverbe, a woman will weepe for pitie to see a gosling goe barefoote'. It is in women's natures to weep at even the natural order of things. This is 'nothing uncomely' but a sign of 'much good nature and meeknes of minde, a most decent propertie for that sexe'. Weeping is not decent for men; is not in their natures; and only occurs when something removes their self-control: 'when they cannot chuse'. When men weep, so Puttenham implies, it will have a significant cause. At the same time, male weeping is closely associated with anxieties about losing and saving face. So male mourning is necessarily associated with self-absorption, with self-watchfulness under the gaze of others.

The gaze of others converges with elegy in interesting ways. Puttenham observes that not only will a weeping man 'turne away' but 'so will the standers by till they have *supprest* such passion' (emphasis added). Male weeping may be so dangerously powerful that it can cause others to lose control. But 'supprest' also implies that mourning is a performance that requires an audience. Male mourning, like the elegist's reluctant entry into language, is closely associated with culturally and socially enforced suppression. As the man who wants to weep publicly, the male elegist has to translate his mourning behaviour into a cultural and social performance that will neither appear 'undecent' for a man nor be misinterpreted as womanly 'meeknes'. The elegist achieves this by invoking previous elegists as respectable role models; and by occupying the literary space that they have made respectable. At the same time, it is the prospect of an audience that simultaneously enables his mourning and ensures it is a 'decent propertie'. In what other ways 'decent' mourning is achieved is the subject of the next section.

ELEGY IN ENGLISH: PERFORMANCE, CONTEST, REWARD AND INHERITANCE

Many of the conventions of male elegy, elegies by men about men, derive from anxieties similar to those in the Puttenham passage. If women's weeping not only comes naturally to them but is prompted by what is natural like a bird without shoes then male grief must always assert its uncommonness. Male grief must perform differences of degree *and* kind. One answer to the supposed 'uncomeliness' of male mourning is to make the elegy itself unnatural and unusual. Many elegies can therefore be read as heroic performances: for example, Daphnis's boast in Theocritus's 'First Idyll' that 'even among the dead Daphnis will serve love ill' (l. 102–3). We have already seen that many elegies begin with protestations of inability. However, lack and the narration of lack become a poetic resource, a means of asserting power and regaining control. 'The last poetic verse is dumb./What shall be said o'er Wordsworth's tomb?' asks Matthew Arnold at the beginning of 'Memorial Verses, April 1850' and then writes 74 lines (Arnold 1959: 226). There is more than a whiff of ludicrous excess about Shelley's 495 lines in 'Adonais'; or about Tennyson claiming that his 'large grief ... /Is given in outline, and no more' and then writing 133 often lengthy sections. Elegy as heroic performance can certainly be traced back to the contest in Theocritus and other ancient pastoral poems. Peter Sacks suggests that this point of origin also informs 'the elegist's need to draw attention, consolingly, to his own surviving powers' (Sacks 1985: 2). This need is often stated in surprising ways. Tennyson asks, as we have noted, who can 'catch the far-off interest of tears' and offers himself and his poem in answer. Immortality is the 'far-off interest' of Shelley's 'Adonais' where the elegist himself is 'borne darkly, fearfully' towards 'the abode where the Eternal are'; and of Gray's 'Elegy' where the poet writes his own epitaph. Auden's observation in 'In Memory of W. B. Yeats' that 'The words of a dead man/Are modified in the guts of the living' is a statement of the poem's own procedures and of the poet's ability to carry them out (Auden 1979: 81).

The statement of surviving power is sometimes more overt: 'Who, if not I, for questing here hath power?' asks Matthew Arnold in 'Thyrsis'. Arnold is unusual in explicitly figuring elegy as quest and he does so because his subject 'on like quest wert bound'. The quest is poetry itself and Thyrsis's words at the end of the poem – 'I wander'd till I died./Roam on; the light we sought is shining still' – not only offer the poet the assurance that all elegists seek but confirm the success of the poem (Arnold 1959: 224–25). 'Sought' picks up on the earlier 'questing' to emphasize that the quest can and must continue. Figuring elegy as quest underlines the heroic nature of the elegiac performance but a quest also evokes such things as the quest for the Holy Grail, an enterprise involving a group of men. The ways in which, to rephrase Auden, the words of dead poets are modified in the guts of living elegies, suggest that references to literary antecedents allow the elegist to claim membership of a band of brothers; to borrow some of their heroism and power; and, like them, bring back something for the benefit of all men. The fact that such references will often be available to only the most expert readers gives them the status of secret signs or perhaps even talismans.

The elegist's heroic assertion of his own power has a surprising consequence: the elegist often places himself in a superior relation to his subject. Three examples are instructive. First, Shelley's 'Preface' to 'Adonais' emphasizes the 'delicate and fragile' nature of Keats's genius, and refers to his 'more penetrable' heart, 'susceptible mind' and 'sensitive spirit'. Keats was simply not strong enough for the everyday brutalities of English literary life. Shelley, in contrast, is able to write a poem that is appropriate to Keats's fragility *and* hold his own with the literary establishment. Second, W. H. Auden's elegy for Yeats uses its subject's poetry against his actual poetics and politics. Finally, Matthew Arnold's 'Thyrsis' is, like Shelley's 'Adonais', a contrast of its author's strength of character with its subject's weaknesses.

The ending of 'Thyrsis' also raises the question of inheritance. Thyrsis's words make clear that the quest is now being passed on to the surviving poet. The elegy has been a kind of test in which he has shown himself worthy of the task: it has earned him the right to imagine hearing Thyrsis's voice. Peter Sacks notes that 'in Greece the right to mourn was ... legally connected to the right to inherit' and that 'ancient law prevented anyone inheriting *unless* he mourned' (Sacks 1985: 37, original emphasis). In this context, we have already noted how Spenser presented himself as the inheritor of both classical and native traditions. Thomas Hardy's elegy for Swinburne imagines a spectral meeting between its subject and Sappho in which the Greek poet calls Swinburne 'Disciple true and warm ... ' (Hardy 1968: 305). Seamus Heaney's elegies 'Casualty' and 'In Memory of Sean O'Riada', referred to earlier, portray their subjects as bestowers on the elegist of special powers and perceptions: 'a rhythm/ Working you' and 'trusting the gift' that produced mackerel 'like a conjured retinue'. In 'A Postcard from North Antrim' Heaney makes Sean Armstrong exemplify the speech of Ulster that he has turned into poetry (Heaney 1979: 24, 29, 20). John Forbes's elegy for fellow Australian poet Martin Johnson 'Lassu in cielo' mocks inheritance by having its subject justify excessive use of garlic by invoking classical authorities (Forbes 1998: 50).

Inheritance is not only about a heroic brotherhood of elegists. Issues of inheritance between male poets inevitably evoke father–son relationships. This is explicit in Heaney's 'Elegy' for Robert Lowell: 'you found the child in me'. Heaney is infantilized by the overpowering masculinity of a poet who '[bullies] out/ ... sonnets' and is at once a gladiator and an armourer. Heaney's reduction happens under the scrutiny of 'the fish-dart of your eyes', and the male gaze that both judges the poet and embodies an order he aspires to appears in other elegies in *Field Work*: 'fisherman's quick eye' and 'a sceptic eye' (Heaney 1979: 32, 21, 29). The male gaze symbolizes a power to which the elegist must submit and prove himself worthy to inherit. In the words of Douglas Dunn's triple elegy for Norman MacCaig, Sorley MacLean and George Mackay Brown, the relationship between elegist and elegized is always that of 'those whom we succeed' (Dunn 2000: 35). The elegist makes himself into a rightful and worthy mourner and thereby, as Kate Lilley points out, 'effects a genealogical consolation' (Lilley 1988: 84).

Matthew Arnold's elegiac poetry is particularly fascinating because it highlights the difficulties of inheritance and survival. Such difficulties arise because, as 'Thyrsis' makes plain, Arnold feels he is writing in a post-elegiac age where tradition has become inoperative: in ancient times 'Some good survivor with his flute would go' and make Pluto himself joyful (Arnold 1959: 222). In his other elegiac poetry, Arnold is, we might say, a very bad survivor and what results is a series of ambivalent encounters with good and bad poetic fathers. Merely to mention another poet is to imply an identification but Arnold is uncertain about what identifications to make. Byron appears in 'Memorial Verses, April 1850' written for Wordsworth as 'the fount of fiery life' who 'taught us little' in contrast to Goethe who was 'Europe's sagest head'. Later in the poem, Arnold hopes for a restoration of 'Goethe's mind *and* Byron's force' (emphasis added) but in 'Haworth Churchyard, April 1855', an elegy for Charlotte and the rest of the Brontës, he is an example of a passionate 'soul' inferior to 'genius ... /Sweet and graceful' (Arnold 1959: 226, 236). Wordsworth and Goethe also appear in 'Stanzas in Memory of the Author of "Obermann"', written in 1849. The former's 'eyes avert their ken/From half of human fate' while the latter's example is too difficult to 'emulate' (Arnold 1959: 255). Most remarkable, perhaps, is 'Heine's Grave', which questions the idea that the elegist's 'fate' is to 'emulate' by turning into a highly critical anti-elegy that rejects the German poet as 'harsh and malign', 'bitter' and 'strange'. 'Rugby Chapel, November 1857', Arnold's elegy for his own father, Thomas, portrays the current age as incapable of inheritance. Thomas Arnold becomes one of 'the noble and great who are gone', 'Servants of God' who will guide 'the host of mankind,/A feeble, wavering line' to 'the city of God' (Arnold 1959: 244, 248, 241–42).

Matthew Arnold's difficulties with good and bad poetic fathers and his portrayal of his own father as a principal agent of mankind's salvation underline the extent to which elegies do as much public as private work. In the first of three *Essays upon Epitaphs* (1810), William Wordsworth examined the origins of grave monuments and epitaphs. The desire to preserve the memory of the dead proceeds, he said, from an individual's ability to 'preconceive' the sorrow caused by his passing and a general belief 'that some part of our nature is imperishable'. Crucially, Wordsworth argued that the wish to be remembered is 'a sensation that does not form itself till the *social* feelings have been developed' (Wordsworth 1810: 50, original emphasis). The interrelation of self and others, individual and community, in remembrance is made explicit in Wordsworth's later characterization of the parish churchyard as 'a visible centre of a community of the living and the dead' (Wordsworth 1810: 56). The idea of community that underwrites Wordsworth's reflections helps to illuminate the relationship of private and public in elegy. The elegist, as we have seen, seeks to deny the commonness of his loss and does so by claiming membership of an elite band of poetic questors and by surpassing what Wordsworth's essay calls 'the general language of humanity as connected with the subject of death' (Wordsworth 1810: 57). At the same time, the elegist must make a monument that is unique but recognizable to others. In this sense, the elegist faces the same dilemma Wordsworth ascribes to the epitaph writer: he must 'give proof that he himself has been moved' while at the same time offering something for 'permanent, and for universal perusal' (Wordsworth 1810: 59). The elegist, in Eric Smith's words, always considers 'two strands of consolation – the memorial and the apotheosis' in order to produce 'the expressive monument' (Smith 1977: 14, 20).

The elegy is therefore simultaneously solid and insubstantial. Milton's 'uncouth swain' calls his poem both 'the meed of some melodious tear' and the counterpart of his own 'destined urn' (Milton 1990: 44, 39). Shelley, typically, invokes monumentality in 'Adonais' in order to reject it. His elegy for Keats is like 'a lucid urn' (XI, l. 91) *and* the graves in the cemetery at Rome which are 'too young as yet/To have outgrown the sorrow which consigned/Its charge' (LI, ll. 451–53). Shelley's lines capture something more of the elegist's particular dilemma in making his grief public. The elegy must offer the consolation of its solid, well-wrought art but it must remain forever 'too young' in order to re-enact and in order for its readers to re-enact the process of that consolation. Wordsworth's 'social feelings' are, to borrow another of his elegant pairings, the 'origin and tendency' (Wordsworth

1810: 51) of remembrance but the elegist must to some extent keep them in action. To borrow Thomas Gray's 'storied urn', the elegy is the urn that is never finally completed but is perpetually being 'storied' in front of an audience.

The elegist's 'social feelings' have other consequences. Tennyson's memorial is at first notional, 'by the measure of my grief/I leave thy greatness to be guessed' (LXXIV), but finally monumental: 'like a statue solid-set/And moulded in colossal calm' (CXXX). What is evoked here is not just a churchyard statue but also a memorial in a city park or square. We have already noted how the elegist seeks to turn a profit from his grief. This may simply be the writing of an elegy which enables him to find consolation. However, it is also the case that many elegists take this profit motive a stage further and seek to extract what might be termed a use value from the deceased which can be returned to the community of the living. I shall discuss this in greater detail in Chapter 6 but it is clear that that part of elegy's public work is to make us reflect on what James E. Young calls in his study of Holocaust memorials 'the consequences of memory' (Young 1993: 11). It is the psychological processes of mourning and remembrance that form the subject of the next chapter.

3

THE WORK OF MOURNING

GRIEF, SELF-POSSESSION AND SELF-FASHIONING

George Puttenham's portrayal of male and female weeping made a clear distinction between 'decent' and 'undecent' mourning. The idea that mourning should be ordered and orderly has been and continues to be crucial to Western societies. For example, in *Crying: The Natural and Cultural History of Tears*, Tom Lutz describes a fact sheet funded by the US Department of Health and Human Services which details the emotions likely to be involved in grief, such as exhaustion, fear, denial and guilt, and the difference between grief and mourning: 'Grief is one's personal experience of loss. Mourning ... is "grief gone public".' These emotions are 'a normal part of the ... process'. Process implies something with a beginning and an end and, in Lutz's words, this 'makes therapeutic sense' in cultures where mourning has been de-ritualized. Individuals and society need to be able to expect an end to mourning (Lutz 1999: 222). As we shall see in the rest of this chapter, the idea that loss leads individuals from initial confusion to regained self-possession has underwritten both psychoanalytical discussions of mourning and literary critical discussions of elegy.

The idea of periods of mourning and appropriate behaviours within such periods is very ancient. For example, the Bible tells us that after the death of Moses the children of Israel mourned for 30 days. Similarly, Jon Davies reports that 3,400-year-old texts from the city of Ugarit refer to lengthy but clearly defined periods of mourning (Davies 1999: 57). The Bible also reports examples of inappropriate mourning behaviour: we find Isaiah complaining about people lingering in cemeteries eating and drinking after the permitted period of mourning. The Romans, too, were concerned with the control of mourning, even specifying periods for particular relatives (Davies 1999: 108, 152). Jon Davies quotes Lucian of Samosata, a writer from the second century CE, who satirized the irrational and overly sentimental nature of burial and mourning beliefs and practices. Lucian was particularly scathing about excessive mourning and myth-derived conceptions of the afterlife. An enormous range of beliefs and practices co-existed in the ancient world but Lucian's satire perhaps underlines that a sense of fictionality where excess can take place is necessary to mourning. We need both a sense of mourning as a period of permitted but contained disorder and a sense that a life story is followed by what we might term a death story.

To return to Puttenham, his distinction between 'decent' and 'undecent' mourning to some extent reproduces an ancient anxiety about proper mourning behaviour. It certainly articulates anxiety about proper mourning behaviour for men. There are many instances of weeping being unmanly in Shakespeare. In *Macbeth*, when MacDuff learns that his entire family has been murdered he says that 'I could play the woman with mine eyes' but resolves to seek immediate revenge, Malcolm comments 'This tune goes manly' (Act IV, Scene III). Similarly, in *Henry V* when Exeter recounts the death of the Duke of York he comments that 'all my mother came into mine eyes/And gave me up to tears' (Act IV, Scene VI). Puttenham's distinction may perhaps reflect the new emphasis that the Reformation brought to funeral arrangements and observances. In the words of Dennis Kay, 'Each ceremony would need to be judged against an idea of "decencie"' while any celebration of the deceased would have to stress their uniqueness in the language of moderation (Kay 1990: 4).

Puttenham's description of both the weeping man *and* the observers turning away also emphasizes that decency and moderation involve significant efforts of self-possession. A classic description of self-possession and of what it is not comes some 200 years later in Wordsworth's autobiographical poem of 1805 *The Prelude*.[1] At the end of Book IV, in what reads like a description of the night scene of canonical elegy, Wordsworth recounts how 'a favourite pleasure' is to walk at night along the deserted 'public way' and then 'slowly [mount] up a steep ascent' (ll. 363–70). On one such excursion, he gains a solitude which brings 'A self-possession felt in every pause/And gentle movement of my frame' (ll. 398–99). Immediately afterwards, he encounters 'an uncouth shape' who seems to him barely alive. The 'shape' turns out to be a recently discharged soldier who is propped motionless against a milestone, 'half-sitting, and half-standing', at first uttering 'murmuring sounds, as if of pain/Or of uneasy thought' and then answering Wordsworth's questions in a voice 'unmoved' (ll. 412, 422–23, 442). Wordsworth directs and accompanies the soldier to a labourer's cottage, noting of the 'ghastly figure' that

> in all he said
> There was a strange half-absence, and a tone
> Of weakness and indifference, as of one
> Remembering the importance of his theme
> But feeling it no longer
>
> (ll. 474–78)

The soldier is obviously exhausted and starving and clearly the opposite of self-possessed. His speech mannerisms seem to confirm that he is disordered in some way. We might even say that his demeanour of nameless loss and 'ghastly mildness' (l. 493) prefigures to some extent Freud's account of the melancholic which we will discuss in detail in the next section. Wordsworth is able to restore his own 'listless sense' (l. 379) and 'exhausted mind' (l. 381); the soldier, when first encountered, is in common parlance literally unable to 'move on'. His behaviour suggests that, in Freud's terms, his mental state is like 'the complex of melancholia' that is 'like an open wound ... emptying the ego until it is totally impoverished' (Freud 1917/1984: 262). Wordsworth's parting entreaty 'that henceforth/He would not linger in the public ways/But ask for timely furtherance and help' (ll. 489–91) further underlines that there are what might be termed 'good' and 'bad' types of solitude, listlessness and exhaustion. One type leads back to the society and the domestic scene; the other remains locked in 'half-absence', mirrored in the inoperative physicality of 'half-sitting, and half-standing'. In the language of Tom Lutz's example, if our listlessness and exhaustion do 'go public' then they should not do so for very long.

Loss and grief, then, are inextricable from anxieties about appropriateness, decency, normality and timeliness. The need to feel that we are in control of the otherness of death and mourning is well illustrated by a more recent anecdote from literary critic Stephen Greenblatt. In an epilogue to his seminal study *Renaissance Self-Fashioning: From More to Shakespeare* (1980), Greenblatt recounts how on a flight from Baltimore to Boston he sat next to a middle-aged man who suddenly began talking about his son who was in hospital in Boston. A disease had taken away the son's ability to speak and his will to live. He could only mouth words soundlessly. His father was worried about his lip-reading skills so he asked Greenblatt to help him practise: would Greenblatt 'mime a few sentences ... Would [he] say, sound-lessly, "I want to die. I want to die"?' This, he believed, was what his son would most want to say to him. Greenblatt tried to help but 'was incapable of finishing the sentence' and in fact refused to (Greenblatt 1980: 255).

Greenblatt traces his incapability and 'resistance' partly to fear that the man might be a homicidal maniac and partly to super-stition (Greenblatt 1980: 256). Crucially, in the context of his book, he was unable to say the words because, he argues, identity is inextricable from choosing what words one says and when; and because articulating a wish to die is 'to let go of one's stubborn hold upon selfhood' and the sustaining illusion that one is 'the principal maker' of that self-hood (Greenblatt 1980: 257). On one level, there is an argument here, as in the Wordsworth passage, about what self-possession is and what it is not. But Greenblatt's resistance can be unpacked a little further. The father's request placed Greenblatt at a crossing point and, as Jacques Derrida has argued in *Aporias*, 'discourse on death . . . contains, among so many other things, a *rhetoric of borders*, a lesson in wisdom concerning the lines that delimit the right of absolute property, the right of property to our own life' (Derrida 1993: 3). Derrida goes on to ask, 'Am I allowed to talk about my death? What does the syntagm [syntactic unit] "my death" mean?' He concludes that it is impossible to attribute to the phrase 'a concept or reality that would constitute the object of an indisputably determining experience' (Derrida 1993: 22). To speak of 'my death' may change how I live if, for example, I am a terminal cancer patient. But I can never be changed by my death in the same way I can be changed by foreign travel, education, a love affair or a job promotion.

This crucial difference converges with the fact that we are used to the words we speak being in J. L. Austin's well-known designation 'performative' (Austin 1962: 25). We say something and it happens and we are bound by it. I say 'I do' and I am married. Greenblatt tells us that he feared that mouthing the father's 'terrible sentence . . . would have the force, as it were, of a legal sentence' (Greenblatt 1980: 256). To speak of death is to evoke and perhaps invite literally nothing. Finally, taking Greenblatt's fear that the father might be a homicidal maniac with Derrida's rhetoric of borders underlines how our conception of death involves a fear that the limits of rationality might be closer and more fragile than we like to think. The father's request invited Greenblatt to cross a border into the inconceivable and the invitation took place in a social context that is detached from any process that would allow a way back. Crucially, Greenblatt's inflight encounter illuminates some of the paradoxes which, W. David Shaw has argued, energize many elegies. First, an elegy is a 'speech act . . . [a] passage from ignorance to knowledge' whose efficacy seems somehow 'guaranteed in advance'. Second, elegists' habitual protestations that their sorrow is unspeakable are a way of implying that their own death is inconceivable (Shaw 1994b: 4–5). Saying 'I want to die' performs neither of those things.

Refusing to say it underlines that we do not want the language we use to talk about death to confront us with what Shaw terms 'the limits of language' (Shaw 1994b: 5).

FREUD: MOURNING AND MELANCHOLIA

William Wordsworth set the discharged soldier on a path that led out of his depressed condition and back to society. Stephen Greenblatt, in contrast, refused to join the distraught father in an activity that risked stepping beyond normative social structures and opening the terrifying opposites of self-fashioning and self-possession. Both responses speak to two anxieties about grief. First, that if grief is left to its own devices, it threatens to become pathological: it ceases to be a response to an event and becomes an all-encompassing disease. Second, that we need a way back from grief to normality. The clearest articulation in the modern period of pathological sorrow and its opposite successful mourning is Sigmund Freud's essay 'Mourning and Melancholia' (1917). It has become a foundational text for the discussion of what Freud terms 'the work of mourning' in both psychoanalysis and literary and cultural criticism. The importance of the essay and, as we shall see in Chapter 5, its continuing controversy can be traced to Freud's establishment of the concepts of 'attachment' and 'detachment' and his distinction between 'normal' and 'pathological'.

It was noted above that Freud portrays melancholia as an 'open wound'. In contrast, successful mourning is a process of healing and return to full health. The work of mourning starts from a recognition that 'the loved object no longer exists' and which 'proceeds to demand that all libido shall be withdrawn from its attachments to that object'. This involves 'great expense of time and cathectic energy' and leads eventually to 'detachment of the libido'. 'Cathectic' derives from 'cathexis', a word coined by Freud's translators to translate the German *Besetzung* ('investment') which describes the amount of energy invested in any attachment, mental process or mental structure. A cathexis is like an electrical charge that moves from one attachment, process or structure to another. Mourning is work because the libido has to be detached from 'each single one of the memories and expectations' bound up with the lost object. Finally, 'when the work of mourning is completed the ego is free and uninhibited again' (Freud 1917/1984: 253). The ego 'is persuaded by the sum of the narcissistic satisfactions it derives from being alive to sever its attachment to the object that has been abolished'. The work of mourning is therefore synonymous with the 'work of severance' (Freud 1917/1984: 265).

In melancholia, the libido is not detached and then re-attached to a new object but 'withdrawn into the ego' where it establishes 'an identification of the ego with the abandoned object' (Freud 1917/1984: 258). This leads to 'narcissistic identification' that in turn leads to 'self-tormenting' (Freud 1917/1984: 260). The loss of the object becomes a loss within the ego: 'In mourning it is the world which has become poor and empty; in melancholia it is the ego itself' (Freud 1917/1984: 254). Robert Pogue Harrison notes two examples in Homer of what might be called 'unworked' mourning leading to melancholic self-abasement (Harrison 2003: 145–6) In *The Iliad*, Achilles withholds the body of Hector from the Trojans. Priam, unable to bury his son, covers himself in filth: 'Dung lay thick/on the head and neck of the aged man, for he had been rolling/in it, he had gathered and smeared it on with his hands' (Book 24, 163–5). Similarly, when Odysseus calls up the dead in *The Odyssey* he learns from his mother's shade not only that she died of heartache at his absence but that his father Laertes wears rags, beds down with labourers by their fire in winter and sleeps on a bed of leaves in his vineyard in summer, all the time yearning for his son's return (Book 11, 202–4).

Freud's essay privileges mourning over melancholia in other ways. Mourning is not only the reaction to the loss of a loved one but is also cast in heroic terms as 'the loss of some abstraction which has taken the place of one, such as one's country, liberty, an ideal, and so on' (Freud 1917/1984: 252). With melancholia, it may even be the case that others cannot perceive the loss or that melancholics are themselves uncertain about what they have lost. Melancholia is first illustrated by the example of 'the case of a betrothed girl who has been jilted' (Freud 1917/1984: 253–4). Indeed, despite a passing reference to Hamlet, Freud's specific examples of melancholia are all female. He tells us that 'a good, capable conscientious woman' is perhaps 'more likely' to become melancholic than one who really is worthless, and uses the example of a woman 'who loudly pities her husband for being tied to such an incapable wife as herself' but is in fact complaining that her husband is incapable (Freud 1917/1984: 255, 257). Melancholia, then, is identified with problems with relationships and self-esteem and made to seem trivial.

The other interesting aspect of Freud's privileging of mourning over melancholia is his use of what he terms 'the economic standpoint' (Freud 1917/1984: 265). Economics enters Freud's essay only two pages in when he notes that just why the long process of mourning and its 'great expense ... should be so extraordinarily painful is not all easy to explain in terms of economics' and goes on to refer to it as a 'painful unpleasure' (Freud 1917/1984: 253). It seems clearly implied here that spending, as our age knows only too well, is a guilty pleasure, and the word 'economic/s' appears throughout the essay. Melancholia, on the other hand, involves 'an accumulation of cathexis' and comes to an end when 'the object has been abandoned as valueless'. Freud also argues that the links between melancholia and mania are partly explained by 'a large expenditure of psychic energy' becoming unnecessary (Freud 1917/1984: 268, 267, 263). Without wanting to make too much of this, normality is made synonymous with normative economic activity and pathology with meanness. As we noted in our survey of elegiac tropes in Chapter 1, the work of mourning involves ideas of expenditure that will bring a return.

FREUD: BEYOND THE PLEASURE PRINCIPLE

'Mourning and Melancholia' is not the only essay by Freud that has proved influential in the discussion of loss. The widely discussed 'fort-da' episode in *Beyond the Pleasure Principle* (1920) shows how the child learns to experience and cope with loss. Freud describes how his 18-month-old grandson, 'a "good boy"' who never cried when his mother left him, engages in a game with a cotton reel whenever his mother leaves the room. He repeatedly throws it over the edge of his cot so that it disappears, at the same time uttering 'a loud, long-drawn-out "o-o-o-o"'. Freud says that this cry represents the German word 'fort' meaning 'gone'. The boy then pulls the reel back into his cot and greets its reappearance 'with a joyful "*da*" ['there']'. There was no doubt, Freud says, 'that the greater pleasure was attached to the second act' (Freud 1917/1984: 284). The 'fort-da' game represents 'the child's great cultural achievement': allowing his mother to leave and then compensating for her absence by 'staging the disappearance and return of the objects within his reach'. The staging allows the child to take an active part in something that initially seems beyond his control and to demonstrate defiance. Repeating the game changes the child's experience from passive to active, and satisfies his desire for revenge (Freud 1920/1984: 285).

As is often the case with Freud, when we look closely at the text we find that obvious things are missing and that his inter-pretation seems limited. For example, Freud's account assumes that the emotional dynamics surrounding the mother's absence are always the same. We don't know if the mother is unhappy at leaving the child or whether the child's behaviour is different if the mother departs having been angry with the child. We might also expect the mother to comfort the child – 'Don't worry, Mummy will be back soon' – but Freud reports no such speech. Similarly, there are a number of ways in which the game can be read, not least that it is a performance. We might even say, following Freud's 'cultural achievement', that it is a work of art and, as such, is open to numerous interpretations. Repetition, as Freud notes, is par-ticularly important. We can add that the repetition of the game turns it into a ritual and that ritual gives order to what might otherwise seem arbitrary and beyond our control. The ritual might guarantee mother's return or it might literally conjure her. 'Fort-da' as ritual not only provides a framework for responding to loss: it also modifies emotions which, if acted upon, would be potentially harmful. The child uses the game both to express and to expel his anger, fear and desire. Finally, the game that is repeated tells us that loss can be, and has to be, dealt with over and over again.

Freud's interpretation ignores the extent to which the 'fort-da' game concerns language and symbols. The game suggests the intimate relationship between language, representation, loss and recovery. For example, many of the tales in Ovid's *Metamorphoses* focus on language at the precise moment of loss of human form or as the articulation of loss. Io, transformed by Jove into a heifer, returns to her father and traces the letters of her name in the dust. Apollo, having caused the death of Hyacinthus, writes his lament, 'AI AI, AI AI', into the petals of the flower that springs from the youth's blood. The beautiful youth is here, gone and then here again in writing (Ovid 1998: 20, 231). The 'fort-da' game therefore demonstrates how language distances us from reality. By using the words *fort* and *da*, the child is using representations of reality and describing a distance between himself and the world. Indeed, the fact that the game is completed by *da* (there) and not 'here' demonstrates this distancing effect.

Crucially, the loss of the mother is played out using a cotton reel that functions as a symbol. Symbols allow us to form conceptions of objects and experiences. Once we have a concept of an object or an experience we can start to gain insight about it. We can think about it when it is not present and we are not involved in it. Mother is someone who goes away and comes back and, by implication, so does everyone else with whom we are in an active relation. Similarly, the game not only enables the child to cope with the absence of the mother: it may also allow him to go on experiencing her while she is absent. In this context, the idea that loss involves severance seems too simplistic. Indeed, the cotton reel seems to function almost in a manner akin to the photographs and objects to which people attach their feelings for lost loved ones.[2]

Peter Middleton draws attention to the sequel to the 'fort-da' game which is less often discussed. The sequel, Freud tells us, was a game in which his grandson

> used to take a toy, if he was angry with it, and throw it on the floor, exclaiming, 'Go to the fwont!' He had heard at that time that his absent father was 'at the front', and was far from regretting his absence; on the contrary he made it quite clear that he had no desire to be disturbed in his sole possession of his mother.
>
> (Freud 1920/1984: 285)

Middleton argues that this indicates that the boy has already learned that being a man involves being 'at the front', that is fighting in the First World War. He goes on to argue that Freud's whole account of the 'fort-da' game portrays 'a strong masculine constellation' – the good boy who never cries, making things go away and come back, and toys symbolizing fathers in danger. The second game changes the meaning of 'gone' to

> having gone off to kill other men and possibly be killed by them. The 'fort-da' game has the war as its subtext; war in which fathers leave sons behind to kill other sons and possibly be killed by them, war which threatens little boys (every departure may bring a death), a threat they learn to master in play.
>
> (Middleton 1992: 91)

Reading this account of the 'fort-da' game with what we have already observed in 'Mourning and Melancholia', it seems clear that Freud portrays loss, to borrow Middleton's phrase, as 'a strong masculine constellation'. War, we might say, guarantees the significance of the game in the same way that mourning is privileged over melancholia because it is just as likely to be caused by what Freud terms 'the loss of some abstraction' as of a loved one. Loss is serious, masculine business.

AFTER FREUD: JOHN BOWLBY

Freud's purpose in making a careful anatomization of the work of mourning was to assist understanding of melancholia or what we would term today clinical depression. John Bowlby observes that Freud's emphasis on depressive illness also meant that there were very few other attempts by psychoanalysts 'to conceptualise the process of grief and mourning ... Until about 1960 only Freud, Melanie Klein, Lindemann, and Edith Jacobson had tackled the problem' (Bowlby 1981: 24). Bowlby's own work in his trilogy *Attachment and Loss* was focused primarily on the importance of the parental relationship in childhood for later mental equilibrium. How we respond to detachment and withdrawal depends on how we come to conceptualize affectional bonds. Simply put, in childhood we learn or don't learn how to lose people.

Bowlby's work is of particular interest for the study of elegy because its starting point is that the dominant psychoanalytic model, derived largely from Freud, is too simplistic to account for 'not only the number and variety of response systems that are engaged [in mourning] but the way in which they tend to conflict with one another' (Bowlby 1981: 31). As we saw in Chapter 1, the range of emotions explored in elegy is too diverse to be accommodated in a model which largely emphasizes what Freud terms the 'work of severance' (Freud 1917/1984: 265). Similarly, Freud's economic model, in which time and cathectic energy are expended to achieve a tangible and beneficial result, cannot explain mourning behaviours that seem to have none at all. For example, the mourner's cry for help often turns into a rejection of help when it is offered.

A detailed consideration of Bowlby's work is far beyond the scope of the present study but there are some aspects of his work that are relevant to elegy. Bowlby's starting point is of particular interest because he sets out to answer points of controversy surrounding the psychological processes of mourning. These include the motivations present in mourning, the role of anger and hatred, the role of identification with the lost person and how we are able to mourn in a non-pathological manner (Bowlby 1981: 25). We do not have to look very far to find that many elegists have been preoccupied with precisely these sorts of questions. So, for example, in 'In Memoriam' we find Tennyson wondering how 'calm despair and wild unrest/[can] be tenants of a single breast,/ Or sorrow such a changeling be?' (XVI) In our own time, 'The Steel', Les Murray's poem in memory of his mother, explores anger, a desire to blame someone for her death and how death confronts us with the limits of human justice (Murray 1992: 189–94). Indeed, as we shall see in Chapter 4, modern elegists have often paid more attention to what Bowlby calls points of controversy than to consolation.

Freud's contention that after the work of mourning, 'the ego becomes free and uninhibited again' (Freud 1917/1984: 253) seems to ignore the fact that bereavement does involve radical change: a husband becomes a widower, a sibling an only child. As Bowlby observes in the context of the loss of a spouse, this 'redefinition of self and situation is no mere release of affect but a cognitive act on which all else turns' (Bowlby 1981: 94). Loss not only involves detachment of the libido: it also effects a conscious change within the ego. Redefinition of self as a cognitive act is central to Ian Gregson's elegy for his gay friend David Platt, 'Animations'. The poem begins by exploring the friendship, 'how my life is swayed by yours/as though by air apparently/still, yet infiltrating'. Knowledge of Platt's death then 'rearranges/ March 21st from your perspective, and its severance', and prompts reflections on how 'continuities of self' and 'slices' of life can ever add up. Platt's lifestyle and his early death seem to shock the poet into a heightened awareness of his conventional family life: 'How does it happen?' (Gregson 2006: 51–3).

Bowlby's work is also extremely useful for the study of elegy in its refinements of the process of mourning into four sometimes overlapping but nonetheless recognizable phases which form 'an overall sequence':

1. Phase of numbing that usually lasts from a few hours to a week and may be interrupted by outbursts of extremely intense distress and/or anger.
2. Phase of yearning and searching for the lost figure lasting some months and sometimes for years.
3. Phase of disorganization and despair.
4. Phase of greater or less degree of reorganization.

(Bowlby 1981: 85)

Of particular interest for elegy is the phase of yearning and searching which, Bowlby notes, other researchers have found to involve restless movement and focusing attention on an environment or part thereof in which the deceased is most likely to be found (Bowlby 1981: 88). This certainly converges with the number of poems written at someone's grave, such as Hart Crane's 'At Melville's Tomb' (1926) or Matthew Sweeney's 'At Plath's Grave' (1989), as this is the place where the person literally is. Crucially, it converges with elegy's return to and re-creation of the primal scene of the relationship between elegist and elegized such as Tennyson's 'dark house' or Arnold's night walk across the Cumnor hills.

AFTER FREUD: JACQUES LACAN

Despite his synthesis of a vast range of theoretical writing, clinical observation and experimental evidence, Bowlby hardly appears in literary-critical accounts of elegy. On the other hand, Jacques Lacan's re-reading of Freud has been found to have wide application. We have already noted that although Freud's discussion of the 'fort-da' game is not focused on language, language is clearly an important aspect of it. Lacan's reading of the game develops it into an account of language acquisition and of the individual's entry into the symbolic order: the order that exists prior to the individual and which she must enter in order to speak and desire. Lacan reads 'fort-da' as a version of 'O/A' so that language acquisition becomes synonymous with 'a pair of sounds modulated on presence and absence' and therefore related 'to the presence and absence of persons and things' (Lacan 1977: 65, 109). The game inserts the child into what we might call the fundamental 0/1 binary code of experience. The symbolic order, the 'place' where adults have their being and where their behaviour is regulated, is inseparable from loss and separation. Loss and separation are the crucial systemic pressures of that order and the 'fort-da' game is about learning that the self is organized and operated upon by those pressures. By repeating 'fort' and 'da' the individual 'becomes engaged in the cycle of the concrete discourse of the environment' (Lacan 1977: 103–4). Loss is simultaneously repudiated and recognized.

Re-reading 'fort-da' as the paired phonemes 'O/A' at the beginning of language acquisition converges with Lacan's observation that 'the subject as such is uncertain because he is divided by the effects of language'. Language, the 'fort' that becomes 'da' only to become 'fort' again, causes the individual to realize himself in the Other because 'he is already pursuing there more than half of himself' (Lacan 1994: 188). The little boy could play with his wooden reel once only, and having retrieved it shout excitedly 'da! da! da!' He continues the game because the reel is simultaneously the mother and the wish for, and possibility of, her return. To continue the game is to keep himself in active relation with her even when she is absent. In the game itself, the mother is exclusively two effects of language: 'fort' and 'da'. The little boy is divided by these effects because he is learning that language is associated with having things and not having them. We might almost say that what he learns from the game is that speech is performative. At the same time, he learns that one can be divided but at the same time survive it and learn to live with it.

IS ELEGY MOURNING?

Psychoanalysis, as Anthony Storr observes, 'is a discipline which explains mental phenomena in terms of historical reconstruction [and] has a vested interest in equating 'deep' with 'early' (Storr 1986: 68). It is easy to see the attractions of a psychoanalytic approach to elegy. Many elegies, canonical and otherwise, are founded on historical reconstruction of the relationship between elegist and elegized subject. Each new elegy writes itself into a pre-existent process of historical reconstruction while writing its own unique version of that process. Similarly, since elegy often employs self-conscious references to earlier examples of the genre, it is an attractive critical task to read for evidence of what might be termed elegy's earliest experiences in later examples.

As we have seen, the writings of Freud, Bowlby and Lacan are all concerned with treating human behaviour in terms of process and structure. A similar concern partly motivates Peter Sacks's 1985 book *The English Elegy: Studies in the Genre from Spenser to Yeats*. Like psychoanalysts, Sacks adopts 'an interpretive (rather than the traditionally descriptive) approach to the genre' (Sacks 1985: xii) but his starting point is scepticism about deconstructionist criticism. For Sacks, '*beginning* with the assumption that an essential lack is already inscribed within language ... risks abandoning a true sense of the experience of loss' (Sacks 1985: xiii, original emphasis). The word 'experience' recurs throughout the opening of the book and the beginning of Chapter 1 finds Sacks asserting that 'elegy *should* be seen as a working through of experience and as a symbolic action' (Sacks 1985: 1, emphasis added). In one sense, Sacks's study prefigures the transition in the history of literary criticism between what might be termed the theoretical period and the return to ethics. This transition seems to have been legitimated by the discovery in 1987 of collabora-tionist articles written during the Second World War by one of the founding fathers of deconstructionist criticism, Paul de Man. Sacks's wish 'to bring out the ... sense of reluctant *process*' inherent in elegy can also be read as a desire to reinstate an ethical subject (Sacks 1985: 329, original emphasis). The fact that this appears in an extensive footnote questioning decon-struction indicates the larger forces that underwrite the book.

Sacks's apparently simple argument may be summarized thus. There is an experience of loss. Language both emerges from this and acts upon it. Language becomes the poem that works through the originating experience and reveals the workings of the mind that wrote it. This raises all sorts of questions about the relation between an actual self and a textual one and about the supposed 'genuineness' or otherwise of literature. It is to Sacks's credit that even if he does not always manage convincing answers to such questions, he doesn't ignore them either. Indeed, all subsequent critics of elegy owe him a large debt. He restores a sense of what Peter Middleton has identified in contemporary elegy as the genre's 'scenes of conflict between exploitation and ethical resistance' and 'the entangled banks of personal history and public culture' that are often evidenced by the elegiac encounter (Middleton 2006: 44, 52). Sacks identifies a huge range of pri-mary and secondary elegiac conventions and reads them as 'lit-erary versions of specific social and psychological practices' (Sacks 1985: 2). As we might expect, Freud appears early on: elegy is literary work and work in 'the sense that underlies Freud's phrase "the work of mourning"' (Sacks 1985: 2, 1). Sacks's primary example of successfully achieving detachment from the deceased and turning back to life is Daphne's metamorphosis into a laurel. Apollo's consolation for her loss is not the tree but that 'My lyre, my locks, my quiver you shall wreathe'. In the words of Ovid's *Metamorphoses*, 'My brow is ever young, my locks unshorn;/So keep your leaves' proud glory ever green' (Ovid 1998: 17–18). In

Sacks's reading, 'Daphne's "turning" into a tree matches Apollo's "turning" from the object of his love to a sign of her. It is this substitutive turn or act of troping that any mourner must perform' (Sacks 1985: 5).

We have already examined elegiac conventions in Chapter 1 and reproducing Sacks's interpretations of all of them is beyond our scope here. Instead, I shall demonstrate the benefits and pitfalls of Sacks's approach with reference to brief examples and offer a comparison of his interpretive approach with an example of the earlier descriptive school. Sacks's approach is typified by his interpretation of elegiac questioning, such as Milton's 'Where were ye, Nymphs ... ?' or John Berryman's questions in elegies for Delmore Schwartz and R. P. Blackmur: 'What final thought/ solaced his fall ... ?' and 'What rhythm shall we use for Richard's death ... /Where will he lie?' (Berryman 1993: 169, 192). In the Freudian model of healthy mourning and pathological melancholy, the mourner is vulnerable to the withdrawal of the libido into the ego and a narcissistic identification with the lost object. Sacks therefore argues that one function of elegiac questioning 'is to set free the energy locked in grief or rage' and reorganize it into 'a voicing of protest'. Sacks continues:

> Most significantly, when the question is addressed to someone else, the mourner succeeds in shifting his focus from the lost object or from himself and turns outward to the world. If tinged with anger, as they often are, such questions actually carry that anger away from its possible attachment to the self – an attachment that, if unbroken, would enmesh the survivor in melancholy. By elegiac questions which often impugn others, the mourner may stave off that self-directed anger.
>
> (Sacks 1985: 22)

This is valuable *and* problematic. Its value lies in the argument that elegiac conventions are not only poets copying their predecessors or submitting to generic models. Indeed, although Sacks does not say so directly, elegiac questioning may partly articulate the sense of reluctant process that is one of his starting points. It is problematic because it elides elegiac questioning and healthy mourning. It is significant that the person asking the elegiac questions here is not the poet but 'the mourner'. Sacks seems to be offering an implicit refinement of Lacan's famous formulation that the unconscious is 'structured like a language' (Lacan 1993: 167) and suggesting that 'an elegy is structured like the unconscious'. This is no longer a literary version of a psychological practice: it is version *as* practice.

Similarly problematic elisions occur throughout the book. Nonetheless, reading poetry as 'the work of mourning' enables Sacks to say much more interesting things about structure, particularly about elegies whose coherence seems at first sight to be problematic. A comparison of his reading of the Urania passage of Shelley's 'Adonais' (stanzas XXII–XXX) and his overall view of the poem with those of one of the better earlier critics of elegy, Eric Smith, shows Sacks at his best. Sacks's starting point is that Shelley's poem is patterned by 'psychological and philosophical currents running deep within [it]' and that these currents result in revisions of elegy's 'inherited fictions' which, in turn, relates to Shelley's wider 'ambivalence toward figurative language' (Sacks 1985: 146). Smith's view is similar but perhaps less sophisticated. 'Adonais' starts as an attempt at conventional pastoral, exceeds its conventions 'and ends by seeming to abandon it in favour of a solution, tenuously connected by idea, but totally outside the fiction [it] has created'. It is notable that Smith goes on to call this a 'structural problem' and quotes Auden's estimate that the poem is a failure (Smith 1977: 58).

Urania, called variously 'mighty Mother', 'melancholy Mother' and 'most musical of mourners', is the initial addressee of the poem. She is, in Sacks's designation, 'the mother-Muse' (Sacks 1985: 165) whom the poet tries to awake in order that she may mourn Adonais and in so doing recognize him as a worthy dweller among 'others more sublime' in 'Fame's serene abode' (ll. 41, 45). When Urania is finally awoken, she rises 'like an autumnal Night' with 'Sorrow and fear ... round her like an atmosphere' (ll. 199, 203, 205), and comes to deliver a speech in the death chamber which begins 'Leave me not!' and 'Stay yet awhile!'; moves to an assertion that 'I would give/All that I am to be as thou now art'; and ends with an image of 'the spirit's awful night' (ll. 222, 232–3, 261). Urania passionately desires a last kiss that 'in my heartless breast and burning brain/ . . . shall all thoughts else survive/ . . . as if it were a part/Of thee, my Adonais!' (ll. 228–32). 'Heartless' means not 'callous' but literally 'unfeeling'.

Sacks reads Urania's speech as exemplifying Freudian melancholia. She is not only unable to detach herself from the lost object: she also wants to internalize the dead Adonais ('as if it were a part/Of thee') and seeks identification with him ('to be as thou now art!'). Although it might seem a little odd to treat Urania as an actual person with an active consciousness, Shelley, in Sacks's view, is able through Urania to objectify the possibility of melancholia; and, as with other delegate mourners in the poem, is able to critique and reject generic conventions about the portrayal of mourning (Sacks 1985: 155–6). In contrast, Eric Smith reads the Urania passage as the penultimate movement of the poem's 'pastoral fantasy' and is more interested in Shelley's reworking of Bion's 'Lament for Adonis' (Smith 1977: 65–6). Indeed, he reads the passage that ends 'I would give/All that I now am . . . ' as a demonstration that 'Urania as chief Muse . . . must retain a connection with the earth in order to offer inspiration'. The final stanza of her speech moving from 'The sun comes forth . . . ' to 'the spirit's awful night' is 'an estimate of the place of the poet in the scheme of things which is the nearest we have yet come to consolation' (Smith 1977: 66). The imagery of the sun giving way to stars prefigures, for Smith, the ending of the poem when Adonais becomes 'a star'.

A comparison of Sacks's and Smith's final estimates of the poem is equally instructive. For Sacks, while 'Adonais' is as much as critique of elegy as an elegy in its own right, at the end 'Shelley has successfully completed much of the work of mourning'. This is a typical Sacks elision of poet and mourner but it allows a persuasive account of the ending of the poem. Shelley's 'success' lies in not only dealing with his grief but also, specifically, in overcoming his own doubts about the genre in order to try and push beyond it (Sacks 1985: 165). The 'star' that is Adonais leads Shelley not to 'pastures new' but to 'the abode where the Eternal are'. For Sacks, the poem 'surely concludes on a suicidal note' (Sacks 1985: 163). However, it must be added that the poem's final 'abode' is surely meant to echo its opening one: 'Fame's serene abode'. It may simply be that the writing of the poem and its achievement in managing to figure its subject as transcendent ensures Shelley's place there. Eric Smith, in contrast, sees 'the final consolation as a culmination of an internal discussion' and argues that

> the poem is better read from the 'dramatic' point of view ... [with the narrator] viewed tentatively as the artist consciously considering the pastoral mode of expression and trying to find consolation within it. Finally, being unable to do so, he abandons pastoral and the Adonis story.
>
> (Smith 1977: 77)

The shortcomings of Smith's approach are made clear by his final observation that 'Adonais' is, surely, imperfect as a complete work of art. Yet we do feel that we are talking of a poem' (Smith 1977: 78). The benefit of Sacks's approach is that he is often able to reveal integrity in works which previous generations of critics have found structurally problematic.

Nonetheless, 'Adonais' is the elegy that reveals most plainly the problems of authenticity that can be summarized by the question: 'is elegy mourning?' Shelley's 'Preface' to the poem makes clear that the poem is as much an attack on contemporary literary-critical culture as a work of mourning. His correspondence suggests his motives were even more complex. Christopher Noble argues that a letter of 29 November 1821 reveals the poem's founding 'political irony', namely 'Shelley's construction of his own poetic persona as resembling Keats's in its "want of popularity" but crucially differing from it "in more important qualities"'. Crucially, an earlier letter of 16 June makes clear that the poem could not withstand too much reality. Having just received 'the heart rending account' of Keats's death, Shelley comments that 'I do not think that if I had seen it before that I could have composed my poem – the enthusiasm of the imagination would have been overpowered by sentiment' (in Noble 2000: 3.6–8). It is difficult for the contemporary reader to re-create a sense of enthusiasm and sentiment as mutually exclusive. Nonetheless, Shelley makes a distinction between something that is worked as opposed to something that is merely felt. This suggests not only that all elegists have to negotiate the relation between enthusiasm and sentiment but also that critics of elegy need to be cautious about reading enthusiasm *as* sentiment.

Peter Sacks's demonstration that most major elegies written before 1900 can be interpreted according to the Freudian 'mourning and melancholia' model inevitably prompts the question of why so few written after that date can be. Similarly, it is virtually impossible to read the substitutive turns or acts of troping repeated throughout a range of twentieth-century elegies. For example, as I have already suggested, one *can* trace a doubled trope of digging and burial that seems to extend from Thomas Hardy's 'Digging on my grave' to Seamus Heaney's 'Digging'. One *could* include in such a tracing the digging in Wilfred Owen's 'Miners'; Douglas Dunn's anxiety that the subject of his book *Elegies* may be 'verbosely buried' in the poetry (Dunn 1985: 9); and John Berryman's rage against his father's suicide expressed as a desire 'to scrabble till I got right down/away under the grass/ and axe the casket open' (Berryman 1993: 406). However, the range of poetries involved and the question of whether some of these poems can properly be called elegies at all suggest that such readings risk seeming opportunistic.

Jahan Ramazani's *Poetry of Mourning: The Modern Elegy from Hardy to Heaney* is a comprehensive attempt to do for the twentieth century what Sacks had done for the canon. Ramazani's argument is that twentieth-century elegists' general antipathy towards the genre's consolatory turn can be read as '"melancholic" mourning – a term I adapt from Freud to distinguish mourning that is unresolved, violent, and ambivalent'. Modern elegist poets 'attack the dead and themselves, their own work and tradition' (Ramazani 1994: 4). The result is that 'the genre develops by feeding off a multitude of new deaths, including the body of its own traditions' (Ramazani 1994: 8). Despite his psychoanalytic starting point, Ramazani is quick to observe that elegy is 'a mimesis of mourning' (Ramazani 1994: 28) and that psychoanalytic vocabulary 'is inevitably reductive' of both generic complexities and 'the multiple kinds of grief' found in modern elegy. Modern elegy is, in fact, 'far from uniformly melancholic' (Ramazani 1994: 30). Modern elegy is ultimately a narrative of the 'repudiation of traditional elegy' whose 'qualifying subplot' of elegy's 'persistence' has become increasingly dominant (Ramazani 1994: 361).

Ramazani's approach converges to some extent with John Hollander's observation that 'the elegiac tone [is] a mood rather than . . . a formal mode' (Hollander 1975: 200). It enables him to deal with an impressively wide range of British and American poetry from Thomas Hardy, Wilfred Owen and Wallace Stevens to Amy Clampitt and Seamus Heaney. At the same time, a narrative that is almost overwhelmed by its subplot and elegies that are anti-consolatory but somehow still elegies are contradictory images that seem about to self-destruct. These contradictions are partly illuminated by something John Berryman wrote in an unfinished story that seems to refer to his father's suicide: 'my desolation and rage over his death persisted, although for years I thought it purely grief' (in Ramazani 1994: 245). There is a satisfaction in being true to one's feelings but this means recognizing that one's feelings have played one false. Suddenly unsettled, the individual is a long way from Wordsworthian self-possession. Without self-possession there is little chance of writing poetry that evokes the possibility of a transformative encounter with language and experience. The self and the poem become abject. In the next chapter, we shall see for ourselves the extent to which modern elegists have sought a balance between the repudiation and persistence of elegy; and how they have often confronted the desolation and rage that accompany grief.

4

'THE NEEDS OF GHOSTS'
MODERN ELEGY

Thom Gunn's prose poem 'Postscript: The Panel' describes a stained-glass panel made by a friend who later died from AIDS. The panel includes an inscription that begins: 'The needs of ghosts embarrass the living.' Gunn goes on to say of the dead that 'Their story, being part of mine, refuses to reach an end' (Gunn 2000: 16). W. David Shaw has argued that 'in their sheer diversity most modern elegies resist explanation by a single controlling idea or metaphor' (Shaw 1994a: 171). This is broadly true but modern elegies have explored a particular convergence of preoccupations that are usefully illuminated by Gunn's poem. The first of these is an emphasis on a continuing relationship between the dead and the living. Many critics have noted modern elegists' unwillingness or refusal to give up their dead and, taking their lead from Freud, have argued for the pre-dominantly melancholic nature of the modern elegy. But Gunn's poem describes something more obvious: it is simply not possible to give up one's dead. Time may reduce the pain of their loss but our dead remain a part of us. Indeed, we can only truly bury our dead when we ourselves are buried. The fact that 'their story' continues with ours goes some way to explaining the auto-biographical emphasis of many modern elegies.

The second important aspect of modern elegy we can derive from Gunn's poem is a concern with number: 'the dead'. It is a concern audible in T. S. Eliot's awestruck observation in 'The Waste Land', 'so many,/I had not thought death had undone so many', and in the opening W. H. Auden's 'In Memory of Sigmund Freud':

> When there are so many we shall have to mourn,
> When grief has been made so public ...
>
> ...
>
> Of whom shall we speak? For every day they die
> Among us, those who were doing us some good ...
>
> (Auden 1979: 91)

In contrast to elegists of the past, the modern elegist has felt obliged to justify writing of a single death in the age of mass deaths. At the same time, this consciousness of other deaths has revealed that the uniqueness of a single death is delusional. For modern elegists, consolation is made even harder to achieve by having to answer the question posed in Mark Doty's poem 'Bill's Story': if we '[live] so separately,/how can we all die the same?' (Doty 1995: 59). The force of Doty's question is perhaps that we just do. Similarly, Elizabeth Bishop's famous villanelle 'One Art' (1976) ends by claiming that 'the art of losing's not to hard to master/ though it may look like (*Write* it!) like disaster'. The things lost in the poem are trivial such as 'door keys', and improbable: 'two rivers, a continent'; but collectively they suggest that living equals losing (Bishop 1983: 178). The bracketed command says that we had better face it. As Jahan Ramazani points out, Bishop's emphasis on loss is indeed emblematic of the way that many twentieth-century poets have portrayed loss as simultaneously horribly simple and simply horrible (Ramazani 1994: 4). Keith Douglas, writing in 1941, imagined himself flayed to a skeleton by 'the processes of earth' and left 'simpler than at birth' (Douglas 1987: 74). Similarly, John Berryman, in one of the poems in

The Dream Songs making up the 'solid block of agony' in response to the death of Delmore Schwartz, mourns 'this complex death' but then reduces it to 'this terrible end, out of which what grows/but an unshaven, dishevelled *corpse?*' (Berryman 1993: 175). Berryman's italicized 'corpse' is, we might say, a literal and poetic dead end beyond which no Tennysonian 'far-off interest' can be earned from tears. To return to Thom Gunn's prose poem, modern elegists have often opted to simplify where their predecessors chose to trope. Loss remains and the elegist's coherence and survival involve the recognition that the dead go on demanding our attention *as the dead* and not as, for example, a Miltonic 'genius of the shore' or a Shelleyan 'star' that 'beacons' from heaven.

Some of the modern elegist's concerns are audible in earlier elegies. For example, Eric Smith notes that with Shelley and Tennyson the efficacy of elegy's 'therapy' begins to 'receive comment' as the elegist starts to watch himself elegizing (Smith 1977: 15). Nonetheless, we should be cautious about subscribing fully to Jahan Ramazani's suggestion that modern elegy can be described by a 'narrative of generic dislocation with a subplot of generic perpetuation' (Ramazani 1994: 10). It might be more correct to say that the scene of elegy becomes too much for the elegist to control. The condition of English poetry at the beginning of the twentieth century certainly suggests that the elegist had been asked to keep too many elements in balance.

PHANTOMS OF FIGURING

C. K. Stead has drawn a detailed picture of early twentieth-century literary culture. The deaths of Swinburne and then George Meredith in the first half of 1909 prompted the *English Review* to observe that 'now indeed the whole Round Table is dissolved' (Stead 1964: 54). English poetry was dominated by critically respected and commercially successful poets like Alfred Noyes, Henry Newbolt and William Watson. Such poets tended to 'sentimentalize and generalize for the sake of a public cause outside the poem' and their poetry was therefore largely nationalistic and militaristic, even jingoistic (Stead 1964: 75). In the words of the novelist Arnold Bennett writing in 1913, 'the sagacious

artist will respect basic national prejudices' (Stead 1964: 48).
Against such a background Thomas Hardy's elegies, particularly
those for his first wife Emma, appear all the more remarkable.

Hardy had already written a poem in 1910 that detached him
from the English elegiac tradition: his elegy for Swinburne 'A
Singer Asleep'. The opening scene of the poem is recognizably
modern: Hardy recalls the first publication of Swinburne's poetry
in 'Victoria's formal middle time' and his own first reading of it
while walking 'down a terraced street'. Crucially, Hardy opens a
new kind of fictional space in the elegy. He invokes Sappho as
not only Swinburne's 'singing-mistress' but also as 'the music-
mother/Of all the tribes that feel in melodies':

VII

And one can hold in thought that nightly here
His phantom may draw down to the water's brim,
And hers come up to meet it, as a dim
Lone shine upon the heaving hydrosphere,
And mariners wonder as they traverse near,
Unknowing of her and him.

(Hardy 1968: 304–5)

Other elegiac scenes, even Milton's pastoralized Cambridge in
'Lycidas', usually have some basis in fact. Hardy's scene is entirely a
product of an individual imagination: 'one can hold in thought'.
Peter Sacks rightly draws attention to 'the aggressive modernity'
of 'hydrosphere' (Sacks 1985: 232). But the line in which it
appears actually conveys very little to the reader of the poem;
and there is a sense in which the scene remains unimaginable
without recourse to a dictionary. Hardy's modern elegiac scene is
also, importantly for the elegiac canon, a feminized one. The
poetic lineage is passed from female to male but it is not passed
on to the elegist himself. At the end of the poem, Hardy tells us
'I leave him, while the daylight gleam declines/Upon the capes
and chines'. Nothing is passed on and there is no consolation.
The broken lineage is discussed explicitly in section VIII which
imagines Swinburne 'sighing to her spectral form:/"O teacher,

where lies thy burning line ... '". Sappho's answer is that Swinburne is her only successor (Hardy 1968: 305).

Hardy's use of 'phantom' and 'spectral' and the poem's emphasis on unveiling the hidden but leaving it largely invisible makes the space he opens in 'A Singer Asleep' recognizable as the realm of the uncanny. In her study of fantastic literature, Rosemary Jackson has noted that the uncanny has both philosophical and psychoanalytic meanings. For Heidegger, the uncanny is the empty space produced by a loss of faith in divine images, a space that is neither God's nor man's. Consequently, religious sense is transformed into myth, magic and the supernatural. For Freud, the uncanny involves uncovering what is usually kept hidden with the result that the everyday is radically defamiliarized. Jackson also draws on the work of Hélène Cixous to argue that the uncanny represents our terror at the possibility of non-being and non-signification (Jackson 1995: 63–66, 68). The eternally recurring, broken conversation between Swinburne and Sappho seems much more akin to Rosemary Jackson's reading of the fantastic than anything we would expect to find in elegy. Swinburne's ghost is forever on the edge of being formed and the poem leaves him forever at the threshold of radical transformation (Jackson 1995: 91). Mourning itself, by implication, becomes an unfinishable conversation.

Imaginary, unfinishable conversations in uncanny elegiac spaces are at the heart of Hardy's poems for his first wife Emma. The group of poems first published in *Poems of 1912–13* commemorate a woman and a wife not a male poet or friend; and do so in a range of forms not a single poem. The uncanny space that was imagined in 'A Singer Asleep' but remained distant and largely unknowable is here let into the poetry. The poems for Emma can be said to function in a similar manner to what Rosemary Jackson reads in fantasy as 'a literature of desire, which seeks that which is experienced as absence or loss' (Jackson 1995: 3–4). The instabilities of the Emma poems derive in part from their oscillation between two aspects of 'a literature of desire': they both *'tell of'* and *'expel'* desire and participate in what she terms an *'opening* activity' which questions the solidity of the real (Jackson 1995: 3–4, 22).

An opening activity and a desire that is simultaneously related and expelled are present in the first poem of the group 'The Going'. It is also worth noting the epigraph to *Poems of 1912–13*: 'Veteris vestigia flammae' is taken from *Aeneid* Book IV where Dido says that her love for Aeneas has rekindled 'the traces of an old flame'. The sequence looks back to the love that preceded the marriage and offers hope of rekindling it but this is an impossibility since one of the people involved is now dead. 'The Going' comprises six stanzas and the first, third and fifth begin with questions: 'Why did you give no hint that night ... ?'; 'Why do you make me leave the house..?'; and 'Why, then, latterly did we not speak ... ?' These have a very different effect from the usual repeated elegiac questions: like 'A Singer Asleep' they picture scenes that exist only in the poet's imagination. In a simultaneous expression and expulsion of desire, Hardy wishes he could, but knows he cannot, follow Emma 'to gain one glimpse of you ever anon'. In stanza 3 Emma is a ghost and in stanza 5 Hardy imagines a rapprochement that never did and never will take place. The opening of uncanny spaces is emphasized by the use of present participles throughout the poem such as yawning and unknowing that give the sense of continuing, unfinished activity. Similarly, Emma's death is 'your great going', then 'your vanishing' and, finally, 'such swift fleeing' which leaves Hardy 'a dead man held on end/To sink down soon ... '. Finding traces of an old flame and trying to rekindle them condemns the poet to continue opening the uncanny spaces and to perpetually invite his own destruction. Indeed, there is almost a sense in which Hardy himself sounds like a dying flame (Hardy 1968: 305–6).

The portrayal of Emma as a ghost is repeated throughout the sequence as is the conjuring of scenes that never happened and at which Hardy was not present. 'Your Last Drive' re-creates a time 'eight days' before Emma's death though she herself was unaware of it. Images such as the 'haloed view' she saw and 'the flickering sheen' of her living face recall the 'dim lone shine' of 'A Singer Asleep' and again underline the poem's convergence with the uncanny. Emma's impending death is similarly underlined: 'the face of the dead', 'one who was not' and 'a last-time look'. There is something macabre and uncomfortably voyeuristic about this and about the words Hardy imagines written on her face, which he wouldn't have been able to read, in stanzas 3 and 4 which begin 'I go hence soon to my resting place ... '. Emma appears to speak the words except that she doesn't and had the scene actually happened she would have been unaware of their presence. In marked contrast to earlier elegists, Hardy seems to be writing not to reassert his continuance and coherence but to recover his inner division and his own absence from his marriage (Hardy 1968: 319).

'The Going' and 'Your Last Drive' also introduce the way that, as Melissa F. Zeiger has observed, the poems for Emma move between the poet's consciousness and that of their subject (Zeiger 1997: 58). For example, in 'The Haunter', spoken by Emma, we read that 'Never he sees my faithful phantom' (Hardy 1968: 324–25). In 'The Phantom Horsewoman' Hardy portrays himself in the third person: 'They say he sees an instant thing/More clear ... A phantom of his own figuring' (Hardy 1968: 332–33). The placing of the same material in different contexts, as if Hardy is uncertain what it looks like or what to say about it, also contributes to the sequence's dual sense of opening and of desire expressed and expelled. There are numerous examples. 'You will not mind' in 'Your Last Drive' becomes 'I did not mind' in 'The Walk'. 'The roomy silence' in 'His Visitor' echoes 'the look of the room' in 'The Walk'. The 'flickering sheen' in 'Your Last Drive' becomes 'her life's sheen' in 'A Dream or No' (Hardy 1968: 319, 320, 326, 327).

The poems therefore haunt each other and add to the sense of division and lack of consolation. The last poem in the sequence 'Where the Picnic Was' remembers a summer outing and a fire: 'the spot still shows/As a burnt circle', and its last stanza begins 'Yes, I am here/Just as last year' (Hardy 1968: 336). Peter Sacks points out the connection between the 'burnt circle' and the epigraph's 'flammae' and clearly wants the ending to be consolatory although he can't quite bring himself to say so directly (Sacks 1985: 259). Jahan Ramazani argues that the 'sequence ... seems to end in despair' but 'really ends in a comforting allusion to Hardy's poetic powers' (Ramazani 1994: 61). However, 'I am here/Just as last year' is hard to read as unambiguous continuity.

The poem recalls an event in the year before Emma's death and the 'just as' could refer to what 'The Going' portrays as unachieved rapprochement. Equally, it reminds us of the ending of 'The Going' with the poet 'a dead man', 'undone' and always about to die finally. The last lines of 'Where the Picnic Was' confront us, rather brutally, with the fact of Emma's death: 'And one – has shut her eyes/For evermore'. 'Shut her eyes' seems to offer the comforting illusion that death is only sleep but the next line snatches it away. The dash portrays not wanting to say what must be said. The last two words echo the last words of 'Beeny Cliff', 'At Castle Boterel' and 'St. Launce's Revisited': 'never more', 'never again' and 'ever into nought' (Hardy 1968: 330, 331, 336). The most that can be said about the ending is that it voices dejected acceptance.

Reading Hardy's poems for Emma together with his elegy for Swinburne suggests that something more complex happened to elegy at the beginning of the twentieth century than a movement away from consolation and towards melancholic mourning. Why does the fabric of the elegiac scene suddenly give way to an uncanny parallel universe? Why does the elegiac impulse suddenly include the fantastic as that which cannot happen and what could not have happened, and seem to founder on something akin to Rosemary Jackson's 'opening activity'? Why is Swinburne's apotheosis figured as something no-one can see? I want to suggest that one way of answering these questions is to read nineteenth-century elegy as a history of elegy's public work being overrun by desire. Elegists have, of course, always had to answer the question of what to do about desire: we might recall here Kate Lilley's observation, quoted in Chapter 2, that 'the elegist spends himself in the service of desire' (Lilley 1988: 51). The elegist's desire can be described in a number of ways. In masculine elegy it is a homosocial or frankly homoerotic desire for the elegized. Melissa Zeiger notes that Tennyson, in old age, was still sufficiently embarrassed by this aspect of 'In Memoriam' to protest that 'If anybody thinks I ever called him [Hallam] "dearest" in his life they are much mistaken, for I never even called him "dear"' (Zeiger 1997: 13). The elegist's desire also involves his own desire for mastery and self-confirmation and desire in the sense of drives that must be restrained or excluded. For example, grief can make the mourner, to borrow Keats's words from 'Ode to a Nightingale', 'half in love with easeful death'.

The public work of elegy, which is often articulated as a strong synthetic drive, enabled desire to be kept in its place: it distracted both the elegist and the reader. Milton's 'Lycidas' is concerned to update classical/mythological pastoral for a Christian audience. Tennyson's 'In Memoriam' seeks to make an emotionally satisfying and practically workable synthesis of contemporary scientific and religious thought. In contrast, Matthew Arnold's numerous elegies are generally unsatisfactory because they articulate a belief that serving, in C. K. Stead's phrase, 'a public cause' is an end in itself. What makes 'Thyrsis' (1867), his elegy for Arthur Hugh Clough, so uncomfortable is that Arnold is unable to extract a use value from Clough's life and death. This is because the story of Clough's life was one of inner turmoil, unfulfilled promise and dangerous flirtation with radical ideas. Clough strayed from acceptable standards of thought and action because he did not have the strength of character to ignore the 'storms that rage outside our happy ground'. Clough, we might say, gave in to desire: 'Thyrsis of his own will went away'. This means that Arnold has to shut Clough safely away inside the landscape of pastoral elegy which is portrayed throughout the poem as foreign, overseas and unreal. 'These English fields ... / ... are not for him./To a boon southern country he is fled/And ... happier air' (ll. 172–76). There is no yearning in that 'happier': it is only so for Clough. What the poem offers ultimately is not consolation but Arnold's celebration of the superiority of his own life choices and of English values. The meaning of Thyrsis's final whisper 'I wandered till I died' is not Clough's desire coming back to haunt the poem: it is all that Arnold wants to hear (Arnold 1959: 220, 224, 225).

In Swinburne's elegy for the French poet Charles Baudelaire, 'Ave atque Vale' (1868), the problem of desire is of a different order. The elegized subject is someone unknown to the poet but a 'brother' poet. The poem makes an intense identification with the temperament of Baudelaire as a writer *of* desire. This is the force of the many uses of the word 'strange'. Baudelaire is the 'sweet strange elder singer' (l. 79) and a 'gardener of strange flowers' (l. 68) whom Apollo mourns with 'strange tears and alien sighs' (l. 151) (Swinburne 1982: 162, 164). 'Strange' is both the desire that Baudelaire's work represents and the elegist's intense desire for the other. One effect of this is that Swinburne's elegy becomes a fantasy of sexual/textual encounter. The elegist's 'flying song' (l. 78) chases after and falls upon the 'shut scroll' (l. 102) of Baudelaire's poetry in what is at once a failed consummation and a masturbatory image. We might also read an allusion to masturbation in the earlier line 'At least I *fill* the place where *white dreams* dwell' (l. 175, emphasis added) (Swinburne 1982: 162, 163, 165). So where 'Thyrsis' performed its own failure to do public work, Swinburne's poem is in part very private work indeed. In this context, the circumstances of the poem's composition are especially interesting. Swinburne began the poem in 1866 after hearing a false report of Baudelaire's death; and didn't publish the poem until 1868, the year after the poet's actual death. What this suggests is that the male elegist is the poet who is particularly primed to respond to death; and is primed to respond to death as the opportunity to write desire. The profession of desire for a dead male subject avoids any risk of reciprocation and of having to negotiate the lived realities of desire.

Writing the elegy *as* desire also means that Swinburne has to try to negotiate what Judith Butler calls 'the quandary of desire in language': 'The circuit of desire pushes the text toward the limits of language in which the name names nothing ... ' (Butler 1995: 381). Examples of naming nothing are numerous: 'alien sighs', the desire to 'wreathe an unseen shrine', Baudelaire's 'irrevocable head' and the 'footless places' of the afterlife (Swinburne 1982: 164, 165, 164). The larger question for Swinburne's poem is whether desire can name anything other than itself. If, as Lacan has argued, desire is always 'the desire for something else', since it is impossible to desire what you already have, then we might expect an elegy-*as*-desire to find apotheosis and consolation especially problematic. Peter Sacks's reading of the poem does not focus on desire *per se* but he usefully draws attention to the fact that one of the principal mourners is 'That obscure Venus of the hollow hill/ ... A ghost, a bitter and luxurious

god' (ll. 158, 162) (Swinburne 1982: 164–65). She is no goddess
of love in the traditional sense but an 'imprisoning seductress'
whose 'hollow hill' is 'the insatiable vacancy that represents
the region of poetic work itself'. And this is just one instance
of the way that Swinburne's poem '[hollows] out . . . all otherwise comforting matrices' (Sacks 1985: 223, 225). Baudelaire's
desire and Baudelaire-*as*-desire cannot outlive themselves: 'And
now no sacred staff shall break in blossom'. Desire can only end
in death and the poem's penultimate stanza asks rhetorically:
'Out of the mystic and mournful garden' where Baudelaire
'Wove the sick flowers of secrecy and shade/ . . . Shall death not
bring us all as thee one day . . . ?' (ll. 180, 182, 186). In the
poem's final stanza Baudelaire is 'now a silent soul', again a
'brother' to whom the poet offers a 'thin . . . wintry' garland; rest
in 'the solemn earth, a fatal mother'; and 'quiet' (ll. 188–98)
(Swinburne 1982: 165).

    First desire, that is in a fundamental sense the impulse to
movement and to action, and to the act of writing; then death;
then nothing. Melissa Zeiger reads the ending of 'Ave atque
Vale' as a moment of 'immobility' or stasis, which is nonetheless
a 'reconfiguration of elegiac motifs' that supplies 'a canonical
template' for much twentieth-century elegy (Zeiger 1997: 41–
42). But this does not answer the question of identity of the
work of mourning once it is revealed as a very private work of
desire. Even a minor poem like Robert Bridges's 'On a Dead
Child' follows a similar movement to Swinburne's elegy. Its
opening words are 'Perfect little body'. It goes on to wonder if
Death has taken the child 'To a world, do I think, that rights the
disaster of this?' but concludes that there is no comfort to be
had: 'in the dark,/Unwilling, alone we embark,/And the things
we have seen and have known and have heard of, fail us' (Bridges
1987: 39–40). The poem moves from the 'perfect little body'
through a fantasized afterlife to the actual darkness of death; it
figures the way that the desire to bring the mystery of death into
language, and to an understanding from the perspective of the
living narrator, to locate and explain it, far from attaining its
object, discovers only the lack on which is it predicated and by
which it is fuelled and driven. In Lacanian terms, desire always

discovers that what is *not known* is in fact what *cannot be known*, and hence that any attempt at explanation is destined to dissolve in failure.

Returning to Hardy, it seems clear that the elegiac scene in his work becomes uncanny precisely because he is prepared to allow desire to do its work: to go on discovering and rediscovering itself as lack. He is unwilling to pretend that the work of desire is the work of mourning or to try and force it to be so. The invisible, 'nightly' meeting between the ghosts of Sappho and Swinburne in 'A Singer Asleep' figures the work of desire: desire keeps on happening, insatiably, eternally, striving to articulate what is beyond language. In the words of the poem, each time we create within ourselves the 'dim lone shine' of desire we can only 'wonder' at but never know what lies beneath it. In this context, the 'Yes, I am here/Just as last year' in 'Where the Picnic Was' (Hardy 1968: 336) is another version of that 'nightly' meeting. But Hardy's elegy for Swinburne and his poems for Emma do more than this. They look for a way through Butler's 'quandary of desire in language' by recognizing that desire in writing is always present either as a trace or as writing itself. This is the source of their self-consciousness as acts of writing. In the poems for Emma, desire is present as a series of impossible texts: the sequence that seeks to perform its epigraph and be traces of an old flame: ashes or burn marks; the visible trace of the sequence's epigraph in 'Where the Picnic Was'; and the writing imagined on Emma's face. The poems for Emma go on reincarnating her as lack; and do so by figuring the process of writing and the process of desire in and as each other. But, in an important sense, that is as far as the poems get. To return to W. David Shaw's paradoxes which we touched on in the previous chapter, the poems for Emma suggest that once the work of desire is allowed to dominate, it is as if the elegist can only ever get to point immediately before the 'passage from ignorance to knowledge' (Shaw 1994b: 4–5). In Hardy's case, as Claire Tomalin's recent biography has shown, the narrator's reviewing of the past has the effect of bringing his dead wife into the present as a revisionary fantasy. The elegist's self remains untransformed. The desire for transformation goes on writing itself.

DEATH'S PROLETARIAT

Uncanny spaces, the elegy as desire, the living about to become corpses and the dead speaking are not present in every modern elegy but they are clearly visible in elegiac responses to the First and Second World Wars. We also find these elements converging with an explicit tendency to write about writing. In one sense, this is the elegist's reluctant submission to language. Tennyson had, for example, worried over the appropriateness of 'modern rhyme' for 'lives . . . Foreshorten'd' and had then written anyway. Modern elegists leave such doubts unassimilated as if to leave the fabric of their poems unfinished. The poetry of Wilfred Owen is a notable instance of how the tendencies we saw in Hardy converge with doubts about writing. In the draft preface to his poems, Owen wrote that 'these elegies are to this generation in no sense consolatory. They may be to the next. All a poet can do today is warn. That is why the true Poets must be truthful' (Owen 1983a: 535). 'They may be' underlines the extent to which Owen's poems are, like Hardy's, impossible texts. Owen is, of course, mocking the reader: the horrors he portrays could never be consolatory. Where Hardy portrayed scenes that never happened or now never could, Owen's impossibility is generic. Like the smashed bodies they portray in unflinching detail, his poems can only be what they are. They are not structures of mourning that lead to consolation. Owen mocks the reader again: a truthful elegy is an oxymoron. The work of elegy can generally be characterized by these lines from Milton's 'Lycidas': 'For so to interpose a little ease,/Let our frail thoughts dally with false surmise.' No wonder Owen abandoned his original idea of calling his book *English Elegies (Owen 1983a: 536).*

   The 'true poets' among which Owen placed himself were not only contemporaries but also canonical figures. As Jahan Ramazani notes, 'Owen's intense engagement with literary tradition enables, not inhibits, his articulation of a new historical reality of untold psychic trauma' (Ramazani 1994: 78). One such engagement takes place in 'Exposure'. The poem's blighted pastoral and portrayal of death-in-life opens with 'Our brains ache', a clear echo of the opening of Keats's 'Ode to a Nightingale', 'My heart aches'. In contrast to Keats's narrator who has often 'been half in love with easeful Death', the collective 'we' for whom Owen speaks have no choice but to 'turn back to our dying'. Similarly, 'The merciless iced east winds that knive us' echo the winds that blow tempestuously and inspirationally through Romantic poetry from Emily Brontë to Shelley. However, these winds are not transformative: at the end of Owen's poem 'nothing happens' (Owen 1983a: 185). In this context, we might revise Ramazani's comment slightly by saying that Owen's articulation of horror and trauma is achieved by taking elements of tradition and rendering them inoperative by showing their limitations. Indeed, his project seems to prefigure Seamus Heaney's intention in our own time 'to take the English lyric and make it eat stuff that it has never eaten before' (in Parker 1993: 123).

What Owen makes elegy 'eat' is three things: pastoral, the fictiveness of its focus on individual death, and the body, specifically young male bodies. We might say that Owen makes the elegy 'eat' its own desires. Pastoral comes into play not only through elegy's origins but because the war takes place in the countryside, the traditional space of retreat in order to achieve heightened consciousness and self-possession. Nature as enactment of pathetic fallacy or as a consolatory space is constantly rejected in the name of being 'truthful'. We have already noted how 'Exposure' presents a dead landscape where 'nothing happens'. The end of the poem also closes off the return which is an inextricable part of pastoral: the soldiers '[glimpse] the sunk fires' and find that 'all [is] closed: on us the doors are closed'. In 'The Show', the poet rises above the countryside and sees a landscape 'cratered like the moon', the abode of caterpillars, worms and 'long-strung creatures' who are 'All migrants from green fields' (Owen 1983a: 155). In the first part of 'Insensibility', we get a typically brusque reminder: 'they are troops who fade, not flowers,/For poets' tearful fooling:/Men, gaps for filling' (Owen 1983a: 145). 'Gaps for filling' is perhaps an oblique riposte to Henry V's famous exhortation to 'close the wall up with our English dead' (Act 3, Scene 1) but it also suggests the men are teeth in the 'long-strung creatures'.

Owen's rejection of elegy's fictiveness takes a number of forms. To return to his comment about his poetry, 'this generation' signals an important turn. The speaker of Owen's poems is usually 'we', the voice of a collective experience. This is immediately problematic because in many poems Owen's collective speakers feel they are already dead. So the usual elegiac address of elegist to elegized is bypassed and Owen's poems are instead addressed to two audiences: first, to the 'we' who speak them; and, second, to 'you', the non-combatants at home. As Jahan Ramazani notes, this reconfigures elegy's usual relationship of 'mourning audience, mourned dead person, and mourning poet. For Owen, the audience is often guilty, the dead person innocent, and the poet split between two poles' (Ramazani 1994: 81). It also means that the endings of Owen's poems are effectively marked 'no exit'. Unlike the endings of, say, Milton's 'Lycidas' or Matthew Arnold's 'Thyrsis', there is no possibility of setting off for 'pastures new' or returning to daily life in 'city-noise'. The poet remains shut inside his experience and the reader shut out. Indeed, readers are presented with more impossibilities: they are asked to mourn losses which they have not experienced directly. In the words of 'Apologia pro Poemate Meo', 'These men are worth/Your tears. You are not worth their merriment'. There is no way for the reader to be worthy 'except [unless] you share' the soldiers' experience (Owen 1983a: 124).

Owen's focus on young male bodies is an answer to what to do about desire in elegy but it also continually poses and answers another question: what is the subject of truthful elegy if not the dead bodies of young men? As Paul Fussell notes in a wide-ranging discussion of homoeroticism in the First World War, 'it is the features of the palpable body that set him off' and around a third of Owen's published work refers to 'boys' or 'lads' (Fussell 1975: 291). The features of the palpable body had been largely absent from canonical elegy even if homoerotic elements were not. Deaths were abroad or bodies were lost. 'Arms and the Boy', about a young soldier and his weapons, portrays a body made for sex and death but not yet involved in either. In a clearly onanistic and voyeuristic image, the poem's narrator imagines the boy '[stroking] these blind, blunt bullet-heads/Which long to nuzzle in the hearts of lads'. The last phrase suggests an international fellowship of young bodies on the brink of being corrupted through being able to corrupt. The end of the poem wants to leave the boy uncorrupted: 'And god will grow no talons at his heels,/Nor antlers through the thickness of his curls' (Owen 1983a: 154). This can be read as a comment on the unnaturalness of weapons but it is also an allusion to Ovid's *Metamorphoses* where the end of desire is so often the death-in-life of transformation out of the human. We might even guess that 'god' is Apollo. In the words of 'Apologia pro Poemate Meo', 'Happy the lad whose mind was never trained' (Owen 1983a: 124). Sex and death are also explicit in this poem where Owen tells us 'I have made fellowships –/Untold of happy lovers in old song' and offers the sado-masochistic image of 'love . . . wound with war's hard wire' and 'Bound with the bandage of the arm that drips'. Sex is also present in 'Disabled' where the wheelchair-bound veteran 'will never feel again how slim/Girls' waists are' and notices 'how the women's eyes/Passed from him to the strong men that were whole' (Owen 1983a: 175).

Owen's focus on the body exemplifies the truthfulness that makes consolation impossible. Bodies that are either not yet fully operative or are completely inoperative fascinate him. By bringing bodies and his own eroticizing of them and of death itself into elegy, Owen certainly asked the genre to digest material it never had access to before but he did something more. Reading Owen's parading of failed consolation back into canonical elegy makes clear the extent to which the genre had been concerned with offering species of national narrative. Milton's attack on the contemporary clergy, Gray's uneasy democratizing and Tennyson's assurance that the most corrosive doubt could still lead back to faith are all examples of this. Owen's bodies, the haunting and accusing dead, and the collective 'we' render elegy finally inoperative as a national and public narrative. We might say that this is the meaning *for the genre* of the famous ending of 'Dulce et Decorum Est': if you could see and hear the realities of death, then 'My friend, you would not tell with such high zest/ . . . The old Lie: Dulce et decorum est / Pro patria mori' (Owen 1983a: 140). It is also the sound of the genre trying and failing to make elegies not out of grief but out of death itself.

By the Second World War, doubts about the functionality of elegy had become a refusal to use it. The title of Dylan Thomas's

'A Refusal to Mourn the Death, by Fire, of a Child in London' (c. 1945) clearly rejects its subject's death as an occasion for patriotism or propaganda. The poem's opening 'Never' opens on to an impossible, uncanny space: the end of time and the poet himself returned to nature. Only then will the poet 'sow my salt seed' and 'any further/Elegy of innocence and youth' would 'blaspheme' the poem's subject. The final stanza shows the child returned to an equally uncanny natural world:

> Deep with the first dead lies London's daughter,
> Robed in the long friends,
> The grains beyond age, the dark veins of her mother,
> . . .
> After the first death there is no other.
>
> (Thomas 1991: 192)

The gnomic/oracular last line 'After the first death, there is no other' may mean that all deaths are the same in that they represent a return to nature. In the context of war, it may also mean all deaths are equally terrible. But there may also be a sense in which there is only actual death not the second death of a 'blasphemous' elegy. The elegist refuses his own desire and the poem's other impossibilities and negatives such as 'I shall not' and 'unmourning' seem to acknowledge that desire can, in Butler's phrase, name nothing.

Hamish Henderson's *Elegies for the Dead in Cyrenaica*, written 1941–47 and published 1948, make similar points. The 'Sixth Elegy' asks 'what requiem can I sing in the ears of the living?' and rejects 'dope of reportage', 'anodyne of statistics' and particularly 'blah about their sacrifice' as 'an insult so outrageous'. What the poet seeks instead are 'words' that 'are worlds of whole love' because 'Other words would be pointless' (Henderson 1990: 33). Elsewhere, Henderson stresses the commonality of death: 'many dead' and 'There were our own, there were the others' (Henderson 1990: 19). Henderson is writing as much about 'the others' as 'our own'. In the 'Third Elegy' the German enemy are 'ourselves out of a mirror' and 'the brothers/in death's proletariat' from which the poem has removed the subtle gradations of the

British class system (Henderson 1990: 21–22). Indeed, the only personal elegies Henderson chooses to write are for the 'seven good Germans' of the 'Seventh Elegy' (Henderson 1990: 34–37).

Henderson's and Thomas's refusals of elegy's conventions typify how many late-twentieth-century elegists have translated the crisis of representation opened by Owen into an explicit struggle with elegy as public work. Writing an elegy risks placing the elegist at the disposal of competing and dubiously truthful discourses – Henderson's 'dope', 'anodyne' and 'blah'. At the same time, the carefully precise title of Thomas's poem prefigures the late-twentieth-century elegist's refusal to submit to the ultimate end of the genre: detachment from the dead. Henderson makes this explicit in the final elegy of his sequence when he writes of the dead that 'their sleep's our unrest, we lie bound in their inferno –/this alliance must be vaunted and affirmed, lest they condemn us!' The poet's job is to 'carry to the living/blood, fire and red flambeaux of death's proletariat' (1990: 45–46).

'OUR WAR CRY'

The remainder of this chapter will not offer a history of elegy in the late twentieth century. Such a history may be had from Jahan Ramazani and others. I will focus instead on two explorations of elegy as public work: breast-cancer elegies and AIDS elegies. These poems demand attention for two reasons. First, the cultural silence that surrounds their subjects makes their answers to elegy's perennial questions such as how to represent absence, or what is an appropriate form for anger, grief *and* consolation especially urgent. Second, as Melissa F. Zeiger observes, AIDS elegies import 'an overriding sense of *shared* catastrophe into the sphere of poetic production' and breast-cancer elegies 'negotiate between individual poetic achievement and the interests of women ... as a class' (Zeiger 1997: 20–21). It is this *assumption* of communality as opposed to earlier elegists' anxieties about it that strikes a new note.

One of the earliest breast-cancer elegies is Adrienne Rich's eight-part sequence 'A Woman Dead in Her Forties', first published in the mid-1970s and collected in her 1978 volume *The*

Dream of a Common Language: Poems 1974–1977. Rich's book opens with a poem about Marie Curie who died 'denying/her wounds came from the same source as her power' and ends with a poem celebrating woman's involvement in nurturing and growth (Rich 1978: 3, 77). Zeiger observes that the breast is 'the prime cultural signifier of womanhood in its sexual and maternal aspects' (Zeiger 1997: 137), so within the frame of the book Rich's poem confronts the question of signification directly in its opening line: 'Your breasts/sliced-off The scars' (Rich 1978: 53). The slash mimics surgery but, combined with the word-sized gaps between the iambs, also suggests that the line can be read as a 'sliced-off' tetrameter. In the remainder of the opening section the subject of the sequence, who is never named, is portrayed among 'half-naked [women] on rocks in sun'. The setting is at once dream-like and mythological: these women might be sirens or sphinxes and are certainly powerfully self-possessed. The subject of the sequence is among them but does not want to show her 'scarred, deleted torso' (Rich 1978: 53). The deleted torso not only echoes the deleted form of the poem's opening line but also evokes other deleted torsos that are usually thought beautiful like the Venus de Milo. Finally, the subject puts her blouse back on with the italicized assertion *'There are things I will not share/ with everyone'*. The section's most metrically regular line is a refusal of communication (Rich 1978: 53).

The first section's portrayal of failing or feeling unable to communicate and of the cancer sufferer's exclusion sets up the rest of the sequence. The poet's reticence is not only personal but also cultural and generational. The rest of the sequence asks what sort of language would be most operative and effective. 'I'm left labouring/with the secrets and the silence/In plain language: I never told you how I loved you' gives way in the final section to 'I want more crazy mourning, more howl, more keening' (Rich 1978: 57, 58). This comes at the end of an inverse progression, from 'neo-protestant tribe' to 'turquoise [beads] from an Egyptian grave', that suggests a journey back to the culturally unmediated roots of mourning. Women wailing are more effective than modern women's culturally learned and sanctioned 'mute loyalty' (Rich 1978: 58). This is then transformed into 'mute and disloyal/because we were afraid': 'I would have touched my fingers/to where your breasts had been/but we never did such things' (Rich 1978: 58). In this context, the word-sized gaps that punctuate the sequence can be read as the difficulty of speaking but also perhaps as the holes left when the unnecessarily and/or conventionally poetic elements are stripped away. The poem's fluid but uneasy relation of free verse and regular metre suggest the difficulty of finding a common language. There is also an echo of Wilfred Owen's accusing ghosts in 'Time after time in dreams you rise/reproachful' (Rich 1978: 57). The unquiet dead signify that the form of the elegy will be unquiet, a perpetual negotiation of the need to speak and of culturally determined silence.

Marilyn Hacker's 1994 volume *Winter Numbers* responds to breast cancer – her own and others – and also to AIDS. There are some interesting convergences with Rich. Rich's 'deleted torso' finds an echo in Hacker's self-description as 'a revised manuscript'; and where Rich is left 'laboring with secrets', Hacker's breasts 'hold/their dirty secrets till their secrets damn/them' (Hacker 1994: 82, 84). Hacker is, however, a very different poet to Rich and the difference lies in her comparative formality. The poems in *Winter Numbers* are largely in dialogue with the sonnet, the corona and the villanelle. Melissa F. Zeiger observes that 'Like the poetry of World War I, these poems detail the inadequacies of traditional elegiac tropes and narratives as a response to massive, general loss' and notes Hacker's punning self-characterization 'cell-shocked' (Zeiger 1997: 159). Hacker's detailing of inadequacies is the consequence of her formal concerns. Where we might imagine that Rich began 'A Woman Dead in her Forties' from the assumption that there was no form for what she wanted to say, Hacker clearly expects form to be operative. Form exists for her not just as poetry but as history. 'Against Elegies' lists the various twentieth-century atrocities and genocides that 'make everyone living a survivor/who will, or won't bear witness for the dead' (Hacker 1994: 14). Hacker also inhabits a particular historical form: her Jewishness. Belonging to what 'August Journal' calls the 'Stubborn people of the Book,/ renewed after ... disappearances' makes it impossible for her *not* to have something to say about survivors, victims and witnesses. Earlier in the same poem she asks 'can any Jew stay indoors with a book/and ruminate upon her own disease,/ . . . absorbed, alone, aloof?' (Hacker 1994: 95, 94).

The refusal to withdraw becomes textual. In 'Against Elegies' Hacker observes that 'The Talmud teaches us we become impure/ when we die . . . once the word/that spoke this life in us has been withdrawn' (Hacker 1994: 14). So where Rich's poetry is lyrical and abstract, Hacker's is narrative and dense with the words we use to speak life. Culture and society are always too ready to withdraw words from breast-cancer and AIDS victims because they are regarded as impure. The poems in *Winter Numbers* are crowded with travel, places, books, music, food, clothes and furniture. In fact, although the book's title evokes metre, one wonders whether it also alludes to the sequential issues of a periodical publication since the poems share so much material with glossy lifestyle magazines. This focus on the material not only celebrates 'the colloquial sublime' (Hacker 1994: 43) in the face of death but also underwrites a deliberate [strategy]: 'Truth, in particulars, I can define' (Hacker 1994: 24). And this is also political, a riposte to cultural stereotyping:

> . . . (the code word, we both know, is 'shrill'
> when some opinionated female won't
> address the 'universal' or keep still.)
> (Hacker 1994: 50)

The piling up of material details and the poems' constant movements between the USA and Europe are a way of writing that avoids both those rules.

Nonetheless, while Hacker's poems resist the universal at the close of a century that has 'made death humanly obscene' (Hacker 1994: 14), her focus on 'truth, in particulars' and her assumption that what she describes is somehow historically determined mean that she is constantly trying to measure the tragedies she describes. 'Each day's obits read as if there's a war on' and yet in response to her own cancer 'I tell myself, it isn't the worst horror./It's not Auschwitz' (Hacker 1994: 76, 83). The search for an operative language runs through the rest of the sonnet sequence 'Cancer Winter': 'I thought/I was a witness, a survivor . . . /I need to find another metaphor' (Hacker 1994: 81). At the end of the sequence, in an echo of Owen's 'these elegies are to this generation in no sense consolatory', Hacker admits that 'These numbers do not sing/your requiems, your elegies, our war cry' (Hacker 1994: 90). The sequence ends 'I woke up, still alive' (Hacker 1994: 90). This is perhaps Hacker's version of the end of Milton's 'Lycidas': 'At last he rose'. As Melissa F. Zeiger points out, in a poem by a woman about other women this rescues the poet and those she commemorates from the 'voiceless . . . preordained place of Eurydice' (Zeiger 1997: 165). It is possible to read this, in Zeiger's words, as '[constituting] a cultural politics as well as a poetics of breast cancer' (Zeiger 1997: 165). However, a book which begins bluntly 'James has cancer. Catherine has cancer./ . . . Whom will I call, and get no answer' (11) ends with 'All I can know is the expanding moment' (Hacker 1994: 95). Hacker's 'numbers' seek to resist the excesses and easements of elegy but seem ultimately unable to find a satisfactory articulation of the collective 'your' or 'our'.

'HOW CAN WE ALL DIE THE SAME?'

Hacker's poems in *Winter Numbers* make clear how elegists in the twentieth century have both felt obliged to articulate a collective experience of loss and found themselves severely challenged in doing so. We might say that both Wilfred Owen and Hamish Henderson struggled with collective articulation because, unlike earlier elegists, they were unable to make a link between death and previous life; indeed, all they had to articulate was collective death. Hacker, similarly, articulates a common death but not a common experience preceding it. AIDS elegies start from a very different position. Melissa F. Zeiger notes that 'the line between the dead and the survivors dissolves' and that 'AIDS is so central a fact in gay consciousness that almost any poem written now by a gay man . . . is likely to include elegiac moments' (Zeiger 1997: 108, 109). Consequently, AIDS elegies tend to perform what she terms 'closural suspension', and the dead often make welcome returns to the mind of the poet and the life of the poem (Zeiger 1997: 108).

Thom Gunn's 1992 collection *The Man with Night Sweats* certainly exhibits some of these characteristics. Indeed, the grieving lover in 'Sacred Heart' drags 'grief from room to room ... /Preserving it from closure' (Gunn 1993: 473). However, it is important to discuss the book as a whole because Gunn employs careful echoings and rewordings of observations about lifestyle on the one hand and of views of the body on the other. So, for example, the comment in part 3 'I said our lives are improvisation' becomes the much starker 'Abandoned incomplete ... / Trapped in unwholeness, I find no escape/Back to the play of constant give and change' (Gunn 1993: 437, 484). Similarly, the 'Blackfoot Indian bone/Persisting in the cheek' that reveals a lover's racial identity becomes the mark of another man's final illness, 'In your cheek/One day appeared the true shape of your bone' (Gunn 1993: 410, 466).

'Closural suspension' is, then, inextricable from gay lifestyle and Gunn sets up an unflinching portrayal of meanings of 'complete' and 'incomplete'. So Allan Noseworthy, the subject of 'Lament', is 'uncompleted as a child' but then finally in death '[achieves his] completeness, in a way' (Gunn 1993: 467, 468). Similarly, the three poems for poet Charlie Hinkle, 'Memory Unsettled', 'The J Car' and 'To a Dead Graduate Student', portray their subject's pain and despair as 'suspended' and 'not ended', and his sexual, professional and creative lives as unfulfilled (Gunn 1993: 479–82). The poet himself is diminished by death: 'Their deaths have left me less defined:/It was their pulsing presence made me clear' (Gunn 1993: 483). Or, in the words of Gunn's final collection *Boss Cupid*, 'Their story, being part of mine, refuses to reach an end' (Gunn 2000: 16).

Deaths that leave the elegist incomplete mean that, unlike canonical elegy, there can be no putting of the self back together because the loss of AIDS is unfinished. Melissa F. Zeiger notes how 'Lament' invokes 'Lycidas' while rejecting the comforts of pastoral (Zeiger 1997: 107). The permanent vulnerability of the gay community to AIDS makes the elegist permanently vulnerable to loss. The final poem of *The Man With Night Sweats*, 'A

Blank', glimpses a former lover who has decided to adopt a child and become a single parent, out with his child: a 'fair-topped organism ... /Its braided muscle grabbing what would serve' (Gunn 1993: 488). We are perhaps back with 'improvisation' here but the depersonalizing and de-gendering of the son and the contingency of 'what would serve' articulate, in Gunn's typically understated way, that there are no templates for gay lives and gay futures just as there are no models for gay loss and gay elegy. There are only 'The variations that I live among' (Gunn 1993: 468). Since 'the dead outnumber us' (Gunn 1993: 485) and all of 'us' are survivors, death itself becomes a 'variation' of living.

Gunn portrays the unbroken connections between living and dead explicitly in 'Death's Door' (Gunn 1993: 485) where the dead watch the living on television, mocking their daily lives and insincere mourning, until snow blows out the set and becomes an empty 'snow-landscape' afterlife. Mark Doty uses a similar image in 'Fog' where a dead boy, summoned by a Ouija board, 'says he can watch us through the television,/asks us to stand before the screen/and kiss' (Doty 1995: 27–30). Snow also appears in Doty's poem 'Chanteuse' where a blizzard fills the lovers' city studio with 'the sudden graceful shock/of being inside the warmest storm' (Doty 1995: 24). Reading this through Gunn might suggest an image of mortality but the location and 'warmest storm' reveal Doty's very different poetic technique and perspective on gay life and death. Gunn's poems quietly insist on variations. The title of 'A Blank' suggests a lifestyle that is being written at the precise moment of seeming to be cancelled out. In contrast, Doty's portrayal of a dangerous but sensual city has the effect of writing gay life and death into the structures of capitalist desire; and of revealing the death drive that is inextricable from that desire. So in 'Demolition' a crowd watches a building coming down because of 'a thirst for watching something fall' (Doty 1995: 1).

We are fascinated and seduced by mortality and decay because they are so deeply imbricated into the world. 'Lament-Heaven' asks

isn't everything so shadowed
    by its own brevity
        we can barely tell the thing

from its elegy? Strip something
    of its mortality, and how do you know
        what's left to see?

(Doty 1995: 72)

Desire, then, is inoperative without loss. At the same time, poetry's concern with becoming and passing away allows it to reclaim particularities that would get lost in the shared currents of desire and mortality. The sister of the woman dying of AIDS in 'Bill's Story' asks 'how can we all die the same?' (Doty 1995: 59). Poetry's role in this is explicitly challenged in 'The Wings' where contemplation of fragments of clothing sewn into an AIDS quilt prompts the observation that 'Embroidered mottoes blend/ into something elegiac but removed;/a shirt can't be remote' (Doty 1995: 38). As all this suggests, Doty's poetry is driven by unresolved tensions derived, for example, from simultaneously asserting that mortality is everywhere and in everything and also the particularity of individual deaths. However, if his poems resist grief and the closure of consolation by portraying death as a brilliant transition, they also have to deal with the question of remembrance. If, as 'Lament-Heaven' has it, the cry at the heart of elegy is *'Oh why aren't I what I wanted to be,/ exempt from history'*, then remembrance must somehow distinguish itself from this generalized feeling of loss.

'Lost in the Stars' recalls an AIDS benefit and a stunning per-formance by a drag queen of the Weill song that gives the poem its title (Doty 2002: 8–12). The poem's setting on 'a midwinter Saturday,/the town muffled by snow' in '1992/[when] we were powerless' portrays a city rendered temporarily inoperative and a community whose marginalization makes suffering even harder to bear. The poem is at once a page from gay history and an elegy for the benefit's organizer, Billy. The poem's answer to its questions 'How will *I* remember them?' and 'how will *we* remember you?' is two-fold (my emphasis). First, the drag queen and her performance are an image of art's ability to convince us, while at the same time reminding us that it is imitation. The observation that 'the limits of flesh/resisted her ambitions' might almost describe the elegist's perpetual falling short of the fact of death (Doty

2002: 9). Second, although the poem ends with the benefit and snow outside 'beyond memory, beyond recovery', a six-line prose coda to the poem tells us that Billy is dead and that Doty has a saucepan in which Billy had made him stew when his own partner died. It concludes that 'the best way to keep something of Billy was to hold on to how much he'd annoyed us: in that way we could remember who he was'.

Gunn's poetry rejects the idea of any final memorial because gay 'lifestyle' is not about final forms. In the context of Doty's portrayal of loss as inextricable from living, a benefit is highly appropriate because it is a kind of memorialization before death. Indeed, a benefit recognizes the inevitably of change and loss even as it seeks to insure against it. It opens on to them rather than seeking to bring them to some sort of closure from which we can move on. In this context, a saucepan and a prose description of the dead person's annoying habits at the end of 142 lines of elegiac, lyrical poetry is perhaps a way of saying that remembrance should be awkward, unassimilable. At the same time, the city is the place of fleeting moments and the only hope the elegist has of capturing them is to use not poetry, the language of the grove, but prose, the language of the city, of its newspapers and obituary notices.

The saucepan updates the cup or bowl that Thyrsis wins for his 'Lament of Daphnis' in Theocritus's 'First Idyll'. What is returned to the city is not what Tennyson termed 'heart's affluence' but an object of practical and nourishing use. But, like Billy himself, his saucepan is an annoyance at the end of lyric poetry. The annoyance might be unpacked as follows. Elegies go on memorializing those tragically dead before their time. However, because we no longer believe in and can no longer figure apotheosis, elegies are unable to put the dead away in some transcendent realm. If apotheosis is possible then the dead don't die in vain; if it isn't then that 'not in vain' has to be translated into something we can use. Billy's saucepan, read back into earlier elegies, figures the uncomfortable necessity of elegiac returns. We might also note here Doty's observation elsewhere 'Better prose/to tell the forms of things' (Doty 1995: 31). Remembrance remains a problematic negotiation with form.

At the same time, the cities of Gunn's and Doty's poems are not the scenes of safe and proper return of the dead. Instead, they are peopled with huge numbers of those who are visibly on the verge of death; peopled, one might say, with traditional elegiac subjects who are, in the words of Gunn's poem 'The J Car', 'Unready, disappointed, unachieved' (Gunn 1993: 481). The use value that can be extracted from gay deaths and from the subversive desire of gay lives is not perhaps one that the city wants. Gunn and Doty, like all elegists before them, insist that their dead have also advanced the unfinished work of the city. Billy's saucepan can perhaps be read both as a refusal to put suffering safely away *and* as an uncomfortable reminder that all inhabitants of the city have a right to what Gillian Rose terms in *Mourning Becomes the Law: Philosophy and Representation* its 'transcendent and representable justice' (Rose 1996: 35).

5

FEMALE ELEGISTS AND FEMINIST READERS

'MY MIND REMAINS'

The previous chapter noted how the elegies of Adrienne Rich
and Marilyn Hacker not only portrayed the suffering and death
of individuals but also spoke to what Melissa F. Zeiger calls 'the
interests of women ... as a class' (Zeiger 1997: 20–21). We also
noted that Rich and Hacker's emphasis on the communality
brought about by breast cancer and AIDS strikes a new note in
late-twentieth-century elegy. However, the idea of female elegy
as a place of exchange as opposed to individual poetic achievement
can be traced back to the early history of the genre. *Hecatodistichon*, published in 1550, comprises 104 sophisticated Latin
distichs paying tribute to the recently deceased Marguerite de
Navarre, author of morality plays and mystical poetry. It was
written by the then adolescent Seymour sisters, Ladies Anne,
Jane and Margaret, who were renowned for their precocious
learning. The work enjoyed something of a vogue in France
where it was translated by Du Bellay and praised by such as

Ronsard but it has only recently been translated into English by Patricia Demers. Demers argues that the emphasis in Marguerite de Navarre's writings on deliverance from the flesh and the wisdom of children would have had an obvious appeal for three 'bookish young women who knew that they were being raised as bluestocking marriage bait' (Demers 1999: 351). The interest of *Hecatodistichon* for the contemporary reader lies not in the precocity of its authors but in its figuring of death as a transformation that allows a continuing relationship between deceased and survivors. In distich 28, Marguerite is made to say: 'My form is dead, and the rest of my body horrible to see, but the beautiful shape of my mind remains' (Demers 1999: 359).

The survival of Marguerite's mind is ensured in part by the Seymour sisters' careful engagement with her ideas so that the tribute performs a shared interiority between elegists and elegized subject. She needs no painterly tributes because, in the words of distich 85, 'she painted and carved herself enough with her own writings'. Although her ultimate destiny is to be bride of Christ, this is in fact 'a second life' (Demers 1999: 363). The distiches are divided between the three Seymour sisters and, while this echoes the procession of mourners common to canonical elegy, its effect is ultimately 'irenic', an accumulation of 'nonviolent yearnings for association with a nurturing maternal figure' (Demers 1999: 354). The fact that all three sisters at some point ventriloquize Marguerite also ensures that she is not inert in language. Marguerite de Navarre is an enduring mentor and not someone to be surpassed through the agonistic contest that elegies often stage.

A feminine elegiac more concerned with attachment than separation and a consolatory turn deriving more from recuperation than from compensatory substitution has been carefully and persuasively reconstructed by feminist critics over the last 20 years. Feminist criticism has also questioned the Freudian model of both mourning and elegy criticism and has introduced a consideration of the differences between male and female psychosexual development. It has also challenged the myths such as those of Apollo and Daphne or Orpheus and Eurydice that have been used to provide tropes for the elegiac encounter. It is this twin project of reconstruction and challenge that I shall explore in this chapter.

The reconstruction of a feminine elegiac derives from Celeste M. Schenck's seminal paper 'Feminism and Deconstruction: Re-Constructing the Elegy'. Her starting point is a recasting of the genre signalled by her opening words 'The female elegist ... '. Elegy is 'a resolutely patriarchal genre' which is better designated 'masculine elegy' because of its focus on male initiation and the writing of 'vocational' poems: 'The masculine elegiac is from the first a gesture of aspiring careerism' (Schenck 1986a: 13–14). The masculine elegy's tradition of novitiate and apprenticeship means that the deceased is '[lifted] ... out of the successor's way'. Such poems therefore '[rehearse] an act of identity that depends upon rupture' (Schenck 1986a: 15). Women, as already noted in Chapter 2, are generally excluded from such poems except as muses or nymphs. This, in turn, has meant that women poets either refuse or have found it difficult to work with the genre's central figures. Schenck notes how early female elegists such as Anne Bradstreet, Katherine Philips and Anne Finch deplore their own inadequacies even more than elegists generally do (Schenck 1986a: 14).

Schenck's point, of course, is not to demonstrate that female elegists have habitually failed when measured against masculine elegy but that they have been and are continuing to do something different:

> To 'meet the case' of a feminine elegiac one would need to raise and answer the following questions: 1) How do women poets understand the elegiac task? 2) How do they invert or suspend traditional elegiac procedures? 3) Which of elegy's rigorously prescribed conventions do they choose to undo or deconstruct? 4) What sorts of poetic solutions emerge in women's funeral poetry that might be termed 'reconstructive' of the genre?
>
> (Schenck 1986a: 14)

The answers to all four questions derive from the fact that female elegists reject the genre's emphasis on rupture and separation and stress connectedness. This is partly because female

elegists generally mourn their personal dead rather than predecessors. Even when female elegists do figure themselves as
inheritors they still emphasize continuity and shared interiority
as we noted in *Hecatodistichon*. Schenck traces this to the fact that
women poets have generally lacked mentors; and to the fact
that female psycho-sexual development and what might be
termed the scene of female identity are 'characterized by continuity
with the mother and an attenuated separation' (Schenck 1986a:
16). The female elegist 'protests final separation by insisting
upon not only the difficulty of severing substantial relations, but
the potential for achieving identity by preserving those very
relations in a kind of continuous present' (Schenck 1986a: 24).

An instructive example of the female elegist's 'continuous
present' is Mary Matilda Betham's eighteenth-century poem 'In
Memory of Mr. Agostino Isola, of Cambridge, Who died on the
5th of June 1797'. The poem is in two 14-line stanzas and one of
11 lines of blank verse. It opens with 'Awake, O Gratitude' and a
rejection of 'selfish Sorrow' and goes on to make a distinction
between grief for 'a tender friend' and both 'a transient pang,/For
worth unknown' and weeping for those 'Whom long acquain-
tance only made me love'. Betham therefore begins with a careful
anatomizing of who should be remembered and how. The sense
of continuing relationship is made clear in the move from first to
second stanza, from 'I/Had once the happiness to call thee friend'
to 'Yes! I once bore that title … '. Although the poem ends
conventionally with 'Long shall we mourn thee! longer will it
be,/"Ere we shall look upon thy like again!"', the bulk of it portrays the friendship founded on a love of poetry, the hope that it
would have continued, and the endurance of Isola's virtues
throughout his life. As in the Seymour sisters' *Hecatodistichon*, the
poem's act of remembrance figures a shared interiority.

Schenck's identification of female elegists' unwillingness to
give up their dead is certainly visible in one of the better recent
anthologies of the poetry of grief *The Long Pale Corridor: Contemporary Poems of Bereavement*. The mother in Paula Meehan's
'Child Burial' imagines turning back time and returning the
child to her womb so 'you would spill from me into the earth/
drop by bright red drop'. The daughter in Eleni Fourtouni's 'The

Sharing-Out' imagines eating and drinking her mother, '[taking] her inside me', so that remembering her is like remembering blood when one cuts one's finger. At the same time, the poem portrays two scenes of looking in the mirror which figure as tropes for a continuing relation between ancestresses and descendants. Similarly, in Jane Draycott's poem for her brother Nigel, 'Search', 'your frightened face sleeps inside mine' (in Benson and Falk, eds, 1996: 153, 166–69, 191). Female elegists' refusal of rupture also means that, in Schenck's words, they imagine 'new or alternative elegiac scenarios that arise from a distinctly feminine psycho-sexual experience' (Schenck 1986a: 18). In the poetry by women in *The Long Pale Corridor*, tropes of bodily re-incorporation of the deceased by the survivor are a constant. Many of these poems also portray returns to the domestic scene as the place where life with the deceased took place and where relationship with them must continue. It would be unwise to generalize too confidently about this but there does seem to be a greater inclination among the anthology's male elegists to reimagine the dead in either idealized or uncanny spaces.

Schenck usefully characterizes such re-incorporations and returns as reversals and undoings of the conventional patterns of elegy. Refusal of rupture also reveals how the transcendence so highly prized in the masculine elegiac is founded on disjunction. She focuses on poems by Anne Sexton and, in particular, on Amy Clampitt's elegy for her mother 'A Procession at Candlemas', to trace these reversals in detail. The scene of the poem is the poet learning that her mother has died in Intensive Care and her journey home along Route 80 where the night-time traffic reminds her of the procession of the poem's title. On close examination, the poem seems less an elegy than an exploration of the question of female origins in contrast to 'the hampered obscurity that has been/for centuries the mumbling lot of women' (Clampitt 1998: 27). 'The mother curtained in Intensive Care' who appears at the start and finish of the poem is an image of this 'obscurity' but her final 'wizened effigy' converges with the 'wizened cult object' of Athene earlier in the poem (Clampitt 1998: 23, 28).

A comparison of Schenck's reading with that offered by Peter Sacks is instructive. Sacks reads Clampitt's poem as articulating 'a typically American desire' for personal revelation. He acknowledges the extent to which Clampitt rewrites elegy by reminding us that the genre generally excludes the maternal and argues that she restores 'a wealth of specifically feminine imagery' to it (Sacks 1985: 323, 321, 324). Nonetheless, because Sacks wants to fit the poem into his consolatory model, he reads the ending of the poem as an example of the work of severance: 'The poem may have sought re-entry to an immediate, unhampered apprehension of the mother's power of origination ... and yet it has closed by hallowing her in and by an inescapable veil' (Sacks 1985: 325). Schenck notes that 'Sacks finds it typical of all elegy to repress the maternal, *and thus*' (emphasis added) identifies Clampitt with a distinctly American and predominantly masculine elegiac. This reads Sacks somewhat against the generosity and subtlety of his reading but his Americanization of Clampitt's elegiac does '[muffle] crucial intertextual resonances' between her poem and the distinctive feminine elegiac Schenck is seeking to reconstruct (Schenck 1986a: 19). For Schenck, Clampitt's careful retracing and re-creation through childhood memories of 'the lost connection' that '[hallows] the wizened effigy' deconstructs the masculine elegiac, replacing disjunction with 'the daughter's psychic return to her mother' and 'recuperation' (Schenck 1986a: 19, 20).

Sacks and Schenck are both alert readers but one feels that in their respective desires to subsume Clampitt's poem into particular elegiacs, neither critic engages with the extent to which the poem remains unsettled. Simply put, Schenck's reading is too positive while Sacks's is too negative. As I have already suggested, Clampitt's poem is as much a poem of self-description as a poem of mourning. The tone of the writing is hopeless, detached and generally depressed as indicated by references to 'the mother'. The poem's structure of 48 tercets in two equal sections causes the reader to re-create the exertions of the journey described and its language exploits both extreme de-realization and elaborate awkwardness to make the journey into a literal transport of emotion. The speaker of the poem seems to use everything that occurs to her and that passes in front of her to think about her mother and her own feelings. The poem therefore offers a mimesis of delusions of reference that adds to a wider sense of secrets being simultaneously revealed and withdrawn.

The final equation of the dead mother with the cult object of a classical virgin goddess simultaneously mythologizes the maternal and renders it unreal and inaccessible. Indeed, placing the dead mother behind a curtain seems to equate her with a medium or oracle who can now never speak and reveal mysteries. The 'lost connection' that hallows the dead mother seems to be rediscovered too late to be read as Schenck's continuity and recuperation. Similarly, the identification of the 'lost connection' with the childhood discovery of a dead bird seems to come dangerously close to equating female subjectivity with melancholic loss. This picks up on the closing image at the end of part 1 where 'wrapped like a papoose into a grief/not merely of the ego, you rediscover almost/the rest-in-peace of the placental coracle' (Clampitt 1998: 25). The equation of female subjectivity with melancholy is something that, as we shall see later in this chapter, feminist critics have fiercely contested.

IS THE FEMALE/FEMININE A LOST OBJECT?

Clampitt's poem ends with 'the sorrow/of things moving back to where they came from': the journey is still in progress so that the destination of 'the mother curtained in Intensive Care' is never actually reached (Clampitt 1998: 28). And one way of reading this is that a search for an origin of the feminine is always doomed to find 'the mother curtained' as yet another version of 'hampered obscurity'. Arrival remains a fantasy. Clampitt confronts this but her poem seems uncertain that rewriting elegy is the best way out of it. This suggests that Schenck's questions about a feminine elegiac can be recast: if there is a feminine elegiac, to what extent is it the result of contestation and to what extent is it the product of the way that the female elegiac subject has been shaped by masculinist constructions? This prompts a further question: how has such shaping limited the materials that female elegists are permitted access to? The case of the early nineteenth-century poet Lucretia Davidson and the cultural construction of her subjectivity throw such questions into sharp relief. In a detailed reading of nineteenth-century critical and elegiac responses to her death, Patrick H. Vincent has shown the extent to which female poetic identity is constructed in terms of 'right' and 'wrong'. I am indebted to Vincent's account for much of what follows although I draw a different conclusion.

Lucretia Davidson (1808–25) was the second daughter of a chronically ill family in which seven of the nine children died young. She wrote poetry from about four years old and was eagerly encouraged by her mother. She died of consumption one month before her seventeenth birthday although some scholars have suggested the cause of death was anorexia nervosa. Her mother gathered her poetry and published it in 1829 in *Amir Khan, and Other Poems*. The book was enthusiastically received by the then Poet Laureate Robert Southey, and Davidson quickly became a stereotypical Romantic heroine. As Patrick H. Vincent observes, Davidson's genius was seen as precocious *and* dangerous and Southey offered an ambiguous warning to parents: 'It is as perilous to repress the ardour of such a mind as to encourage it.' Southey's article also emphasized the self-sacrificing nature of Davidson's life and death (Vincent 2003: 4). Female genius is simultaneously as inimitable as any type of genius *and* self-consuming and therefore a bad example to other young women. Southey's article was translated into French and Russian and Davidson's work remained in circulation for several decades particularly when it was republished in 1841 along with the literary remains of her sister Margaret (1823–38) who also died from consumption and who, their mother claimed, had assumed Lucretia's 'poetic mantle'.

Vincent notes how Lucretia's 'career [was] constructed and marketed as that of a real life Corinne', the eponymous tragic poetess heroine of Mme de Staël's novel of 1807. Lucretia Davidson inspired two elegies, published 13 years apart, which, in Vincent's words, address 'the vexed issue of a poetess's self-sacrifice' and therefore 'give us valuable insight into women poets' different strategies of literary transmission and authorization' (Vincent 2003: 8). France's leading woman poet, Marceline Desbordes-Valmore, published 'To Lucretia Davidson, young American dead at 17' in 1832. The poem is notable for the portrayal in its closing stanzas of a number of sister artists and the resultant emphasis on women poets finding identity through group solidarity. Davidson might have been able to avoid her untimely end if she had come to France and encountered such a female community. At the same time, Vincent argues, Desbordes-Valmore's poem equates Davidson's death with suicide and 'with a patriarchal society which isolates women from each other' (Vincent 2003: 12).

The Russian poet Karolina Pavlova published 'Three Souls' in 1845. The poem offers an equation between three women poets: French poet Delphine Gay, Lucretia Davidson and Pavlova herself. In marked contrast to Desbordes-Valmore's poem, Pavlova is determinedly unsentimental and portrays Davidson as a lonely, alienated genius. Her early death was the result of not being prepared to fulfil her Romantic destiny that would have required her to go on suffering in order to write verse. She is now 'an angel of truth'. Pavlova, in contrast, has been 'assigned a peaceful path' and 'Majestic dreams [shine] in her' (Vincent 2003: 10). As in Schenck's reading of the masculine elegiac, Davidson has been lifted 'out of nature, out of the poem, and out of the successor's way' (Schenck 1986a: 15). Pavlova, Vincent argues, wanted 'to be taken seriously, to be remembered as a poet and not simply as a "poetess"' but her strategy seems to have backfired. Male critics called Pavlova and her verse 'muzhestvenii' (masculine) and she was later criticized 'for being overly insensitive to her estranged husband and for not attending her father's funeral' (Vincent 2003: 12).

The case of Lucretia Davidson and the two very different elegies for her show the difficulties surrounding both the literary portrayal of female subjectivity and female forms of literary transmission. The two early attempts at the revaluation of Davidson outside the stereotype of Romantic heroine were equally problematic. Marceline Desbordes-Valmore's poem offered Davidson a hypothetical salvation by writing her into a putative and untransacted community of female artists that exists outside the canon. Karolina Pavlova attempted to elegize Davidson in terms of the masculine elegiac but in doing so placed herself outside predominant constructions of feminine subjectivity. As with the case of Sylvia Plath in our own time, Davidson's subjectivity and literary value are synonymous with loss and self-sacrifice. And because loss and self-sacrifice are culturally ambivalent markers, they can be endlessly contested and manipulated. Like Plath, Davidson stood for her immediate contemporaries at the limits of the permissible. What she represented was simultaneously desired and feared. And, also like Plath, the interpretations of her life and career reveal the extent to which the cultural production of female subjectivity is often an unstable mix of stereotype and fantasy.

REGENDERING MYTH, RECONSTRUCTING GENDER CODES

Female subjectivity returns us to the question that dominates the final section of Amy Clampitt's 'A Procession of Candlemas', 'Where is it?' In the context of this discussion, 'it' is the female/ feminine, its articulation and its place. Indeed, 'A Procession of Candlemas' seems to be written at a point of tension between the search and desire for an originating identity and the mourning of it as a lost possibility without ever resolving or even ameliorating what produces that tension. If one accepts that the poem is simultaneously trying to produce something and threatening it then it is hardly surprising that what 'A Procession at Candlemas' ultimately produces is fantasy. In one sense, this fantasy is the imagined return to the mother that never actually takes place but, in another sense, it is the range of contradictory female identities that the poem seems equally invested in including such as virgins, undutiful daughters and women in patriarchal societies.

Clampitt's poem seems haunted by these presences from other times and places. In the context of elegy as a genre women have usually been portrayed as species of ghosts, whether unreal nymphs and powers in Milton and Shelley or the phantom Sappho in Hardy's poem for Swinburne 'A Singer Asleep'. Feminist criticism generally has sought an answer to 'Where is it?' that challenges ideas of fantasy, haunting and lack. In re-reading elegy, feminist critics have focused on three main areas. First, in

Schenck's formulation, they have continued to see whether it is possible to '"meet the case" of a feminine elegiac'. Second, they have examined the extent to which dominant Freudian models of elegy criticism reproduce the genre's patriarchy. Finally, they have challenged the construction of the female by both genre and criticism and sought to unpack its masculinist assumptions. In the remainder of this chapter, I will survey the most decisive interventions by feminist critics.

Peter Sacks starts his discussion of the origins of elegy with myth and one of the most interesting feminist interventions also starts with a re-reading of the place of myth in the genre. Melissa F. Zeiger's *Beyond Consolation: Death, Sexuality and the Changing Shapes of Elegy* (1997) is centred on the story of Orpheus and Eurydice, which 'has served as a template – a structural paradigm, even an ominous, self-fulfilling prophecy – for elegiac production' and is 'a nexus of often contradictory, anxiety-creating impulses central to poetic production' (Zeiger 1997: 2, 13). Zeiger's sense of nexus and contradiction leads her to take issue not only with Freudian models of mourning, or what she terms 'heroic male narratives of renunciation' (Zeiger 1997: 4), of which Sacks's book began a process of normalization. She also takes issue with Sacks's derivation of successful mourning from the story of Apollo and Daphne. For Zeiger, focusing on Apollo's lost love, which was actually something close to a thwarted rape attempt, and on his successful substitution of part of the metamorphosed Daphne for it, is highly problematic. For Zeiger, the Orpheus story is visible throughout the genre in ways that the Apollo and Daphne story is not.

Sacks, in fact, largely dismisses the Orpheus story. Orpheus is an 'equivocal' figure, 'an unsuccessful mourner' and therefore 'a negative model for the elegist [because he] insists on rescuing his *actual* wife rather than a figure or a substitute for her'. It is Orpheus's failure in Freudian terms to find a new attachment that leads to his destruction. He refuses 'to turn away from or to trope the dead' (Sacks 1985: 72). This seems highly selective. As the story is told in Ovid's *Metamorphoses* it might be argued that Orpheus does to some extent trope his loss by telling of others' love and loss. Another reading is, of course, that Orpheus's love for young 'tender boys ... /The brief springtime' is a way of avoiding loss altogether. Zeiger's reading of the importance of the Orpheus story for elegy argues that many of its elements such as the turning away from women to young boys and Orpheus's eventual destruction by the Maenads seem to prefigure aspects of elegy including fear of, or anger against, women; a tension between homoerotic desire and heterosexual norms; and the erotic nature of desire to reconnect with or disconnect from the dead.

The Orpheus story, then, reveals the sexual imaginary at work in elegy and, crucially, raises the question of what woman's place and roles are in the genre. Zeiger notes, for example, that Milton's 'Lycidas' begins with a reference to Orpheus's destruction by the murderous Maenads and argues that this '[creates] a world of opposition that magnifies the poet's struggle' (Zeiger 1997: 8). At the same time, Orphean motifs work to emphasize the success of the poem itself. The second loss of Eurydice led to a second flowering of Orpheus's poetic power and his eventual death and dismemberment led to the apotheosis of his poetic voice. The death of Edward King is the occasion of the poem and its success is inextricable from his own successful apotheosis as 'the genius of the shore'. Zeiger also argues that the Orpheus myth 'haunts elegy as a potent shadow-text even when not overtly invoked' (Zeiger 1997: 9). So, in 'Adonais' Shelley figures Keats as Orpheus *and* Eurydice; and in 'Thyrsis' Arnold makes Clough stand in for Eurydice: 'Some good survivor with his flute would go/ ... And flute his friend, like Orpheus, from the dead' (Arnold 1959: 222). It is Clough's supposed failures that feminize him and this, in turn, leads to a need to portray women as absences: 'from the sign is gone Sybilla's name', the Proserpine whose foot 'never stirred' the Oxford countryside, and the girl who used to work the locks but is no longer there. Arnold's success, in contrast, is identified with 'the world and wave of men', that is safe from the classical world with its temptations and sexual ambivalences.

As I argued in Chapter 4, the case of Hardy's poems for his first wife Emma is more complex. Emma functions as what might be termed a living or present absence. Zeiger is particularly alert to the way the poems move between the poet's consciousness and that of their subject (Zeiger 1997: 58). The point at issue for a feminist reading of the poems is the extent to which Hardy gives a space for the articulation of a female voice and the extent to which that space is made and controlled by him. In 'The Haunter', spoken by Emma, we read that 'Never he sees my faithful phantom' but in 'The Phantom Horsewoman' Hardy portrays himself in the third person: 'They say he sees ... / ... A phantom of his own figuring.' Being a phantom in Hardy's poems is perhaps little better than being an effigy in Clampitt's elegy: its effect is to place the woman both inside and outside the text. For Zeiger, Hardy '[suspends] the woman in a feminine space defined as exterior to the process of cultural production: in short, the place of Eurydice' (Zeiger 1997: 61).

Zeiger's reading of how twentieth-century female elegists have challenged Orphean motifs and reworked Eurydicean ones acknowledges the importance of Celeste Schenck's observation of recuperation instead of severance, but also argues that female elegists sometimes do give up their dead, do engage with the genre's careerist occupation and do open a dialogue with the elegiac canon. Women's elegy therefore brings into and holds open the question of whether or not to substitute the poem for the deceased. Zeiger surveys a huge range of female elegists including H. D., Edna St. Vincent Millay, Muriel Rukeyser, Sylvia Plath, Anne Sexton, Elizabeth Bishop, and contemporary poets Rachel Blau DuPlessis and Ruth Stone. Her conclusion is that, cumulatively, as in Elizabeth Bishop's elegy for Robert Lowell 'North Haven' which reads nature as a cycle of 'repeat, repeat, repeat; revise, revise, revise', women elegists 'insist on tirelessly revisionary practices of reading and writing rather than on the need to institute any homogenous paradigm' (Zeiger 1997: 82).

The emphasis on revisionary reading and writing is persuasive but one wants to add that twentieth-century female elegy is often more disruptive because it reintroduces the corpse and the scene of the grave into the genre. In this context, Clampitt's mother 'already lying dead' is merely the least graphic manifestation of a wider trend. One effect of this is, as Zeiger notes of Anne Sexton's 'The Truth the Dead Know', is to make the dead 'undead objects of desire and continuing agency' (Zeiger 1997: 80). Sexton's 'truth' is, of course, recognizable from personal experience. 'What would X say if she were alive to see that', or, 'I'm sure that's what Y would have wanted', we say to ourselves. At the same time, bringing the corpse into the poem produces a number of other effects. First, by figuring continuing relations, affectionate or otherwise, with corpses, female elegists risk offering us inversions of the positivities of kinship and existence. Second, leaving the corpse in the poem and, indeed, often ending the poem with it, suggests that mourning is unfinished and unfinishable. It also suggests an unwillingness to accept the fact of death by leaving the body figuratively and textually unburied. Finally, leaving the corpse in the poem tends, as we saw in Clampitt's poem, to place individuation under question.

In the case of inversion, it may well be the case that those positivities need their inversions in order to be fully mobilized by an awareness of their threatening opposites but because poems are usually linear they risk figuring inversions as desirable destinations and positive goals. The questions of individuation and of unfinished and unfinishable mourning are much more complex but some fascinating answers are suggested by evidence from clinical practice. In her paper 'Does Mourning Become Electra? Oedipal and Separation-Individuation Issues in a Woman's Loss of Her Mother', Helen Meyers argues that when the mother dies a woman experiences 'a greater internal change involving a sense of having lost part of oneself' and 'there may or may not be the expected aspects of mourning' (in Akhtar, ed., 2001: 20). Meyers reviews three clinical examples: Case 1, a successful, happily married woman who lost her mother at 50; Case 2, a woman who had a conflicted relationship with her mother who died when she was in her early 40s; and Case 3, a woman in her 20s, a survivor of abuse by her stepfather who, on the death of her mother, left a marriage and an academic career to become a 'high-class prostitute' (in Akhtar, ed., 2001: 21–27).

Meyers uses these three examples to critique both Freud and John Bowlby and argue that while many people do go through all or some of the work of mourning to resolve their loss, 'many others ... do not and come out none the worse for wear' (in

Akhtar, ed., 2001: 28). In Case 1, the woman adopted the social activities, behaviours and even the posture of the mother although she exhibited no depression or change in mood. In Case 2, the woman seemed relieved at the death of her mother, took over her mother's art store, found renewed energy for and achieved success with art practice of her own, and experienced greater sexual freedom. In Case 3, the woman's prostitution activity was revenge against her mother for not confronting the stepfather's abuse and for having middle-class ambitions for her. She believed that her mother had sold herself and her daughter to the stepfather (in Akhtar, ed., 2001: 27). In all three cases, the lost object remained internalized. None of the women seems to have gone through the process of mourning in which feelings are gradually withdrawn from the lost loved one so that the mourner 'gets over' her loss. In contrast, each woman 'became' the woman she imagined her mother to have been. In Cases 1 and 2, Meyers argues that 'there was a sense of loss of part of the self that was resolved and filled in by internalization and unconscious identification of the self with the mother'. This produced internal changes that led to 'a strengthened and now more complete self-concept' (in Akhtar, ed., 2001: 29). One feels bound to add that the evidence as Meyers reports it leaves one uncertain whether the responses to the mothers' deaths in Cases 1 and 2 might have been as much defensive as adaptive, avoiding the pain of mourning instead of confronting it. One is also left wondering 'what happened next?' For example, did the 'more complete self-concept' last or did it also turn out to be a stage in a longer process of mourning? Returning to the corpses in female elegies, however, it seems likely that they figure the internalization discussed by Meyers. They perhaps point to a yearning for the possibility of and potential for adaptive loss even if they don't always achieve it.

The other important contribution by feminist critics has been the re-reading and reconceptualization of Freud. Juliana Schiesari's *The Gendering of Melancholia: Feminism, Psychoanalysis, and the Symbolics of Loss in Renaissance Literature* offers a detailed re-reading of 'Mourning and Melancholia' by placing it in a long tradition of writing from the Renaissance onwards that privileges the male melancholic as an artistic and intellectual type. What

she terms the 'crystallization' of Freud's essay around the figure
of Hamlet reveals 'a tacit but highly demonstrable admiration'
for this view of melancholia. Freud's 'admiration' is demonstrated
by his insistence that melancholia involves heightened self-criti-
cism and dissatisfaction with the ego on moral grounds. These
are less 'the effects of a turbulent unconscious than of an over-
developed superego' (Schiesari 1992: 5). Freud's reference to
Hamlet reveals, she argues, his indebtedness to conceptions of
homo melancholius as especially gifted and blessed with special
access to Truth.

We have already noted in Chapter 3 how Freud privileged
mourning over melancholia and how, at first sight, his gendering
of melancholia seems to work in the opposite direction to the
main thrust of Schiesari's argument. The passage in question runs
as follows:

> [The patient] really is as lacking in interest and as incapable of love
> and achievement as he says. But that, as we know, is secondary;
> it is the effect of the internal work which is consuming his ego –
> work which is unknown to us but which is comparable to the
> work of mourning. He also seems to us justified in certain other self-
> accusations; it is merely that he has a keener eye for the truth than
> other people who are not melancholic. When in his heightened
> self-criticism he describes himself as petty, egoistic, dishonest, lack-
> ing in independence, one whose sole aim has been to hide the
> weaknesses of his own nature, it may be, so far as we know, that he
> has come pretty near to understanding himself; we can only wonder
> why a man has to be ill before he can be accessible to a truth of this
> kind. For there can be no doubt that if anyone holds and expresses
> to others an opinion of himself such as this (an opinion which
> Hamlet held both of himself and of everyone else), he is ill, whether
> he is speaking the truth or whether he is being more or less unfair to
> himself. Nor is it difficult to see that there is no correspondence
> between the degree of self-abasement and its real justification.
>
> (Freud 1917/1984: 255)

Freud's description of what the patient presents is completed
by a footnote to the Hamlet reference which quotes his remark to

Polonius in Act II, Scene 2 that 'Use every man after his desert, and who shall scape whipping?'

The passage is, to say the least, confused. One of the most striking things about it is the ease with which Freud first elides the patient speaking the truth as it appears to him with the possibility that he may in fact be speaking the truth: 'he has come pretty near to understanding himself'. This has the effect of suggesting that male subjectivity – and it *is* male since the passage continues with a comparison between male and female melancholics – involves a melancholic self-loathing which must be kept under control but which is also, it is implied, a potential source of insight: 'it may be'. Male subjectivity, we might almost say, always involves feelings of worthlessness. Freud then seems to step back from this possibility by reminding himself and his readers that the patient is ill no matter what he is saying; and that there is no relation between the patient's apparent self-knowledge and his real self.

Reading this from Schiesari's perspective, it seems that Freud is trying to reconcile the two ways in which melancholia has been viewed: as pathological on the one hand, and as cultural apotheosis on the other. However, it is less certain that a single reference to Hamlet reveals a desire to go on privileging male melancholia; and I think it is possible to read the relevant passage from 'Mourning and Melancholia' in a very different way. Ideas of degeneration and deviancy had been very influential in late-nineteenth-century Europe. The Italian criminologist and psychiatrist Cesare Lombroso had not only popularized the idea of the born criminal distinguishable by physiognomic features or deformities but had also argued in *L'uomo di genio in rapporto alla psichiatria* (*The Man of Genius*) (1889) that genius was a species of hereditary mental illness. Similarly, the Hungarian physician and social critic Max Nordau, a follower of Lombroso, had argued in *Entartung* (*Degeneration*) (1892) that European civilization was degenerating. Furthermore, he interpreted the works of such diverse writers as Baudelaire, Nietzsche, Tolstoy and Wagner as the products of a physiologically visible pathology.

We now regard such ideas as pseudo-science but they were widely accepted as serious medical diagnoses. Freud had dismissed degeneracy in his 'Three Essays on Sexuality' (1905) with the observation that it had become fashionable 'to regard any symptom ... not obviously due to trauma or infection as a sign of degeneracy'. He added that 'It may well be asked whether an attribution of "degeneracy" is of any value or adds anything to our knowledge' (Freud 1991: 48–49). In the context of degeneracy the passage from 'Mourning and Melancholia' looks partly like Freud's attempt to make melancholia pathological in a scientifically credible way. The reference to Hamlet functions not as Schiesari's 'tacit but demonstrable admiration' for *homo melancholius* but as a tacit dismissal of the idea that there is, to use Freud's term, any real 'correspondence' between the alienated, artistic temperament symbolized by Shakespeare's character and mental illness. Freud's 'For there can be no doubt ... ' seems designed to lift melancholy decisively out of the cultural realm and into the pathological one. Just as the passage draws back from saying that male subjectivity is intimate with self-loathing, so it also draws back from the well-established equation of illness with insight. It is almost as if we can see Freud realizing that he is being seduced by dominant conceptions of melancholy.

The Hamlet passage, then, invites a number of readings but for Schiesari and other feminist critics the greater difficulty lies in where 'Mourning and Melancholia' leaves female subjectivity. As we saw in Chapter 3, Freud regenders melancholia in order to deprivilege it and reduces it to the status of magazine problem-page issues with relationships and self-esteem. Crucially, in Freud's writings, the pathological is generally synonymous with the female/feminine. As Kaja Silverman observes in *The Acoustic Mirror: The Female Voice in Psychoanalysis and Cinema*, Freud's essay has the effect of making melancholia 'the norm for the female subject ... which blights her relations with both herself and her culture' (Silverman 1988: 155). Reproducing the detailed readings of theorists of female subjectivity such as Luce Irigaray and Julia Kristeva offered by both Schiesari and Silverman is outside the scope of this study. However, if, as we saw as far back as George Puttenham (see Chapter 2, p. 28), female mourning can be dismissed as the appropriate sign of women's humble, pious and naturally submissive natures, then elegy

becomes an important ground for the revaluing of female subjectivity. For example, tears are largely absent from modern
women's elegies because weeping is not only a prelude to the
final severance in masculine elegiac but is also a devalued form of
female behaviour.

The challenge for the female elegist is, therefore, two-fold:
how to find a way of writing loss that reproduces neither the
masculine elegiac nor the inferior melancholic subject position
left by Freud's distinction. We have already noted an emphasis in
both female elegies and feminist criticism on continuing rela-
tionality between survivor and deceased. Louise O. Fradenburg's
important paper '"Voice Memorial": Loss and Reparation in
Chaucer's Poetry' offers another approach to this by contesting
Freud's concept of substitution developed in 'Mourning and
Melancholia' and in his discussion of the 'fort-da' game in *Beyond
the Pleasure Principle*. Fradenburg notes that Freud frequently
asserts that the loved object is never really given up and quotes
from his 1929 letter to Ludwig Binswanger:

> Although we know that after such a loss the acute state of mourning
> will subside, we also know we shall remain inconsolable and will
> never find a substitute. No matter what may fill the gap, even if it be
> filled completely, it nevertheless remains something else. And, actu-
> ally, this is how it should be, it is the only way of perpetuating that
> love which we do not want to relinquish.
>
> (In Fradenburg 1990: 182)

This is very different from the idea in 'Mourning and Melancholia' that 'the work of mourning is completed' and that the
ego eventually severs its attachment from the lost object (Freud
1917/1984: 253, 265). There can be no substitution because the
particularity of the lost object is unique and cannot be repeated.
Mourning can therefore never be completed: it can only 'subside'.

Substitution, then, starts to look less and less likely as a conclusion because it is in fact a form of defence against loss; and
defence can only be a process not an outcome. This is important
because substitution has been central to theories of mourning
and to criticism of elegy (Fradenburg 1990: 182). This has

obscured 'both the nature of attachment and the nature of loss' and 'our understanding of the elegy' (Fradenburg 1990: 183). The impossibility of substitution also prompts a re-reading of the 'fort-da' game in 'Beyond the Pleasure Principle'. As already noted in Chapter 3, the meaning of the game may actually be more complex than Freud's reading of it as mastery-through-substitution allows. Fradenburg argues that the thread in the game can be read relationally:

> ... what if *fort* and *da* are not so much alternating oppositions but particularities linked by this thread? What if *fort* and *da*, that is, are particularities in the same way that 'mommy' and 'me' have been discovered to be? ... Freud's little child ... may be creating something new – a gestural meaning, something like 'there is a thread between this and that' ...
>
> (Fradenburg 1990: 183)

Allowing the possibility of 'something new' helps to clarify not only the extent to which relatedness depends on particularity but also 'why metaphors of "subjection" or "submission" to language, prominent in Lacanian theory and in [Peter] Sacks's account of elegy, may require some interrogation' (Fradenburg 1990: 183).

The point of Fradenburg's interrogation is to expose 'the authoritarian rhetoric' involved in such accounts. Submission and subjection, like substitution, seem to have little to do with the work of mourning and its insistence on healthy grieving:

> When 'health' is defined as submission to the rule of law, a subjection for which we are to be compensated by figures that transcend immortality and individuality, then we need a political reading of the elegy, of theories of the elegy, and of elegiac theory.
>
> (Fradenburg 1990: 184)

The political reading she proposes would be especially alert to three aspects of elegy and elegy criticism. First, the idea that the elegist 'submits' to the genre means that 'elegy *creates* and *produces* authority *as* external, inevitable ... Elegies construct power'. Second, elegy criticism's extensive use, since Peter Sacks, of psychoanalytic concepts has the effect of distancing the genre from politics and society. We can add to Fradenburg's point that the encounter between elegist and subject and between critic and elegy is often made to seem as private and isolated as the therapeutic encounter between analyst and analysand; and that, historically, psychoanalysis has signally failed to take account of the wider cultural, economic and social relations from which analysands present their difficulties. Finally, adapting Fradenburg's critique, we can observe that elegy criticism has, until fairly recently, been dominated by a masculine 'hermeneutics of transcendence'. If we accept the implications of Freud's rejection of substitution and severance, then we can perhaps start to see lost objects as 'irreducible particularities' (Fradenburg 1990: 184, 185, 193).

6

AFTER MOURNING: VIRTUAL BODIES, APORIAS AND THE WORK OF DREAD

The revaluation of female elegists and feminist critiques of male elegy and its male critics have introduced proper notes of hesitation and provisionality into thinking about the work of mourning and the elegiac performance. There is a range of other critical and philosophical writing that offers further challenges to dominant ideas of elegy and mourning. Four aspects of this writing will be explored in this chapter.

Catherine Waldby's study of the Visible Human Project (VHP), although not concerned directly with elegy and mourning, shows how virtual technologies, such as digital imaging of the human interior, highlight the complex currents of cultural meaning that flow between living and dead bodies. Waldby's explorations of 'the biomedical imaginary' (Waldby 2000: 136–37), the way that medical science's claims to pure logic involve an unacknowledged reliance on fantasies and mythologies, illuminate elegy in startling ways. Jacques Derrida's work in *Aporias* and *The Work of Mourning* is equally illuminating in its explorations of the limits of thought and of how to bear witness to the uniqueness of individuals. The English philosopher Gillian Rose sought fresh perspectives on the body politic and the relation between mourning and the foundation of law. Her work suggests that the city in elegy may be a fruitful area for further study. Finally, Christopher S. Noble's work on nineteenth-century English elegy argues that all recent accounts of elegy reproduce Freud's work of mourning and offers a new theoretical model: the work of dread.

VIRTUAL BODIES

The US National Library of Medicine at Bethesda authored the Visible Human Project (VHP) in the mid-1990s. The corpses of an executed murderer, Joseph Paul Jernigan, and an unnamed 59-year-old woman who had died of a heart attack were used to produce virtual male and female bodies. The corpses were first scanned in an MRI machine. They were then frozen in blue gelatine at −85° C and cut into four sections that were CT and MRI scanned. Finally, the frozen sections were placed in a dis-section machine called a cryomacrotome and sliced 1mm at a time. After each slice, the remaining cross-section was digitally photographed: 'In this way the corpse was converted into a visual archive, a digital copy in the form of a series of planar images' (Waldby 2000: 14). The male and female bodies were translated into data capable of infinite manipulation.

The VHP seems, at first sight, far removed from elegy. However, Waldby shows how the VHP's fascination derives in large part from how it rewrites the meanings of life and death and redraws their limits. It is this rewriting and redrawing that can be read back into elegy. Waldby notes how the VHP 'enacts the proposition that the interface between virtual and actual space, the screen itself, is permeable, rather than a hygienic and abso-lute division' (Waldby 2000: 5). The result is a 'new interiority, a projected space of private, psychic being made globally visible' (Waldby 2000: 6). Elegies can also be read as virtual spaces not only in the older literary sense of 'a product of the imagination' but also in the computational sense of things that mimic their 'real' equivalents. Elegies are generally concerned to portray a living person and their exemplary actions and qualities when alive. Such portrayals often compress and fold time and space in a manner akin to the hypermedia links and 'flythroughs' of virtual technology. Auden's elegy for Yeats, for example, places its subject in a virtual landscape composed of real and symbolic elements. More to the point, elegies are particularly concerned to portray their subjects' interiority, a kind of authentic psychic being, and to enact a species of permeability. The elegy, we might say, acts as a screen on which the subject appears and through which their being and their voice passes back into the world of the living.

The enacted permeability of the actual screen in the VHP and of the screen of the poem in elegy makes revelation possible. Elegists reveal the elegized to their readers and their own regained or new found coherence to themselves. Such revelation is, as Waldby reminds us, closely related to Heidegger's concept of *poiēsis* or a making present of things. Heidegger's observation, in *The Question Concerning Technology and Other Essays*, that 'modern technology is a challenging which puts to nature the unreasonable demand that it supply energy that can be extracted and stored as such' might also, like the VHP, seem remote from elegy (in Waldby 2000: 28–29). However, it points to how both anatomy and elegy rely on the actualities of death in order to model life. If we consider that elegy, like medicine, derives from dead bodies then elegy itself, in its consolatory turn, starts to look like a species of medicine and one that is particularly concerned with hygiene and healing. Waldby's comment that 'Anatomy involves finding a use-value for the corpse, calling it to account in order to produce a surplus of vivification for the living' (Waldby 2000: 51) might just as well be applied to elegy. Indeed, there may be some fruitful work to be done on the rise of anatomy and elegy in the sixteenth century. Andreas Vesalius's *De Humani Corporis Fabrica Libri Septem* (*Seven Books on the Structure of the Human Body*), widely celebrated as the beginning of modern medicine, was published in 1543. We might ask whether elegy, in its canonical sense, starts to be writeable at the same time as early modern anatomical scientists begin to map the body.

Waldby reminds us that the importance of Vesalius's book derives precisely from it being a book: 'the form of the book suggests *both* a spatiality and a temporality' (Waldby 2000: 64).

Another interesting convergence of anatomy and elegy is to be found in Waldby's discussion of 'exscription'. She uses the term to describe 'a writing out of the bodily interior' as projectable images (Waldby 2000: 96). The elegiac performance is also an exscription of this type, a writing out of a no longer available interiority and subjectivity. We can also consider the meaning of the term in the work of French philosopher Jean-Luc Nancy. George Van Den Abbeele calls exscription in Nancy's thought a writing practice 'that *exposes* philosophical thought to its unheard of outside *in* the very act of speaking the end of philosophical thought as the internal limit to its sense' (Van Den Abbeele 1997: 14). In this context, anatomy and elegy are forms of exploration and knowledge that can only occur when a limit, such as the change from life to death, has been reached. Elegy, like anatomy, initially relies on the fact of a corpse or, to borrow Waldby's words, 'an anatomical body from which the complications and open-endedness of subjectivity and vitality have been subtracted' (Waldby 2000: 23). However, unlike anatomists, elegists often have to account for the complicated subjectivities of their subjects. The annoying Billy in Mark Doty's 'Lost in the Stars' (see Chapter 4) is the internal limit of the poem's sense and can only be memorialized in a prose coda. Similarly, the complications of Clough's life cannot be assimilated into Matthew Arnold's 'Thyrsis'. Clough is shut away into a classical pastoral and only allowed back into the poem's English scene as a nostalgic whispering voice.

The VHP also prompts ontological questions that can fruitfully lead into a reconsideration of elegy: What form is death? What form is a dead body? The VHP, Waldby argues, becomes an 'iconic form ... taken out of organic time, the time of death and decomposition' and 'made amenable to the virtual time ... of storage, retrieval'. What results is 'an impossible temporality' in which information is reversible and susceptible to infinite repetition and reformulation (Waldby 2000: 129). In this context, we can say that while elegy charts a progress from loss to consolation, from loss of speech to restored coherence, it is also permanently available to repeat that progress. However, to suggest that the elegist is in effect a species of virtual automaton who repeats an elegiac performance for each new reader would be a crude reduction of the reading process. Like the VHP, elegy is not only amenable to the storage and retrieval of its processes and consolatory progress but, crucially, to their reformulation by new readers and writers. Extrapolating a little further from Waldby's discussion of temporality, we can add that the temporality of elegy, like that of the VHP, is also 'palindromic' in that it can be read backwards and forwards (Waldby 2000: 130). The elegy reads backwards from the separation of elegist and elegized. E. A. Markham figures this literally in his elegy for Geoffrey Adkins: 'As there's no good place to start let me walk/backwards till, [I bump] into you' (Markham 2002: 82). The elegy then reads forwards from that meeting to their separation, and then further forwards into an imagined afterlife. Elegy always risks that final act of reading forwards into an imagined future whereby the separation is either transcended or transmuted into some new relation.

The two final areas of Waldby's discussion of the VHP that illuminate elegy are, first, the management of interpretation, and, second, the body as social text. Waldby uses Michelle Le Doeuff's work on the interpretation of imagery in philosophical texts as a starting point for the first of these. Such imagery, Le Doeuff argues,

> is inseparable from ... the sensitive points of an intellectual venture ... the meaning conveyed by images works both for and against the system that deploys them. *For*, because they sustain something which the system cannot itself justify, but which is nevertheless needed for its proper working. *Against*, for the same reason ... their meaning is incompatible with the system's possibilities.
>
> (In Waldby 2000: 137)

Theocritus's 'First Idyll', which elegizes a subject who is at first silent, then rejects poetry and song and finally invokes a disruption of the natural order, is framed by a singing contest whose prize is an intricately worked cup showing images of young love, strength in old age and general fruitfulness. Auden's elegy for Yeats portrays its subject's body in images of 'provinces', 'squares', 'suburb', 'current' and 'cities' but it does so to offer Yeats as a restorative example in a contemporary political context. The dead poet and 'the free man' are linked as political bodies. In Waldby's terms, the 'use value' of Yeats's corpse is that it can be viewed as a body politic.

The management of interpretation is a crucial part of elegy because elegy itself needs this ability to manage its subject. As Drew Leder observes of mechanistic models of the body,

> while the body remains a living ecstasis it is never fully caught in the web of causal explanation ... Yet the living body is that which always projects beyond such a perspective. Its movements are responses to a perceived world and a desired future, born of meaning ...
>
> (In Waldby 2000: 145)

Death reduces the subject of an elegy to a finite, readable system. The body can no longer give birth to any new meanings of itself. Any new meanings that are produced are the work of the elegist responding to the way death limits the body's spatiality and temporality and to the dead body, in Julia Kristeva's words, as 'the most sickening of wastes ... the utmost of abjection ... death infecting life ... [that] beckons to us and ends up engulfing us' (Kristeva 1982: 3–4). For some elegists, an important aspect of the elegiac performance would seem to be almost a welcoming of the corpse in order to make it into a consoling art object. Shelley's 'Adonais' portrays its subject's 'leprous corpse' (l. 72) that also 'Exhales itself in flowers' (l. 173). The corpse as art object is central to Seamus Heaney's eroticized female bog corpses: the nipples like 'amber beads' in 'Punishment' and the body as 'perishable treasure' in 'Strange Fruit' (Heaney 1975: 30, 32). In contrast, as noted in Chapter 4, for other elegists such as Wilfred Owen and John Berryman, it is precisely the corpse as abject that reveals the limits of meaning and of the management of interpretation.

Waldby argues that the VHP challenges the dominant Western humanist ideas of 'the human body as a social surface produced

by subjective depth' and as a product of an 'unknowable interiority' (Waldby 2000: 159). To some extent, elegy clearly
converges with such conceptualizing of the body. It is audible in
Theocritus's 'First Idyll' where Daphnis's silent grief remains
incomprehensible to his questioners and is never satisfactorily
explained by Daphnis himself. However, elegy reveals the extent
to which Waldby overstates her case. A huge range of elegies
from Tennyson's 'In Memoriam' and Arnold's 'Thyrsis' to Seamus
Heaney's poems in *Field Work* and Thom Gunn's in *The Man
with Night Sweats* make a powerful argument about the relationship between sociality and subjecthood. In terms of the poems,
Tennyson and Hallam, say, or Heaney and Sean Armstrong produce each other as subjects through their interaction as social
actors. Indeed, to use Waldby's terms, elegies constantly surprise
us with how much can be read about 'subjective depth' on a
'social surface'. Of course, the elegiac has to be re-conceived as
social text in order that death is somehow acceptable and the
corpse put in its proper place. At the same time, elegies show us
that sociality converges with an interiority that is not only
knowable but, in an important sense, shared.

MOURNING BECOMES THE LAW

The proper place of corpses and the relation of that place to the
social and political aspects of mourning and, by extension, of
elegy are further illuminated by the work of the philosopher
Gillian Rose. In *Mourning Becomes the Law: Philosophy and Representation* (1996) she argues that our practices of death and
mourning are ethical practices and therefore emblematic of what
she argues is a risk at the heart of 'learning, growth and knowledge': the 'constant risk of positing and failing and positing
again' which she calls "'activity beyond activity'" (Rose 1996:
13). A key part of Rose's discussion centres on Nicolas Poussin's
painting of 1648 *Landscape with the ashes of Phocion*.[1] The source
for Poussin's painting and our knowledge of its story is Plutarch's *Life of Phocion*. Phocion was an Athenian general and sta-
tesman, renowned for speaking with 'austere and commanding
brevity', whose life was a model of virtuous action. He fell

victim to political plotting, was found guilty of treason and sentenced to die, like Socrates, by drinking poison. Plutarch continues: 'The malice of Phocion's enemies went further; his dead body was excluded from burial within the boundaries of the country, and none of the Athenians could light a funeral pile to burn the corpse ... ' (Plutarch 1959: 231). Phocion's body was removed and cremated outside the city walls by a man paid to do so. Poussin's painting shows the next part of the story. Phocion's unnamed widow raised an empty tomb on the site of his cremation and took the ashes – Plutarch actually says 'bones' – home under cover of darkness. She buried them 'by the fireside in her house' with the following dedication: 'Blessed hearth ... protect and restore [his remains] to the sepulchre of his fathers, when the Athenians return to their right minds.' Plutarch's story concludes with this very fact: the Athenians erected a statue in Phocion's honour and buried his bones 'honourably at the public charge' (Plutarch 1959: 233).

Poussin focuses on Phocion's widow gathering her husband's ashes. His painting depicts Athens as a combination of classical architecture and pastoral scene. In the background and middle ground, figures in classical dress are engaged in cultural and sporting activities: archery, literature and music. In the foreground, in the shade of a large tree, Phocion's widow gathers his ashes while, behind her, a servant looks back at the city fearful of discovery. The action of the painting not only takes place outside the city but also, as the background activities suggest, outside culture. No contests can be staged in Phocion's honour or songs and poetry composed and performed in his memory.

Rose takes issue with established interpretations of Poussin's painting as the opposition of 'the act of redeeming love to the implacable domination of architectural and political order' (Rose 1996: 25). For Rose, the politics of the painting are more complex: the gathering of the ashes protests not against order *per se* but against aberrant power. Phocion's wife and her maidservant enact the justice that the city is temporarily unable to (Rose 1996: 26). The continuing life of the city as embodied in its continuing enactment of justice relies on the proper recognition of loss. For Rose, 'By insisting on the right and rites of mourning', Phocion's

widow, like the heroine of one of Western literature's foundational works, Antigone, performs a species of the 'activity beyond
activity' that Rose argues is crucial to the work of reason and to
the inner life of the individual. It is worth quoting Rose at
length here:

> To acknowledge and to re-experience the justice and injustice of the
> partner's life and death is to accept the law, it is not to transgress it –
> mourning becomes the law. Mourning draws on transcendent but
> representable justice, which makes the suffering of immediate
> experience visible and speakable. When completed, mourning returns
> the soul to the city, renewed and reinvigorated for participation, ready
> to take on the difficulties and injustices of the existing city.
>
> (Rose 1996: 35–36)

Leaving aside any dealings one might have with the criminal-
justice system, death is the event that makes 'visible and speak-
able' every individual's contract with the city. The deceased and
the survivors are put into an active relation with the city's legal
systems: registration of death, certificates for legal burial, reading
of wills, division of estates. The city offers this to all its citizens
and at the same time allows the survivors time and space in
which to mourn. In this way, the rupture of death is assimilated
into the life of the city.

Death, then, in Rose's terms, 'renews' the city because it
reveals that the city and the society it encloses are composed of
the living and the dead. As Philippe Ariès observes, 'the dead have
gone through the moment of change, and their monuments are
the visible sign of the permanence of their city' (Ariès 1976: 74).
In the words of Abraham Lincoln's famous address at Gettysburg
cemetery: 'It is for us the living ... to be dedicated here to the
unfinished work which they who fought here have thus far nobly
advanced ... [and] to the great task remaining before us' (in
Harrison 2003: 27–30). The burial of the dead within the city's
walls is the city's recognition that its story is unfinished but
continuable. The reburial of Phocion and his commemoration with
a statue not only represent the Athenians coming to their senses:
the city transcends a particular historical moment to reaffirm its

enduring power and values. Death, the greatest rupture in the rational order, cannot be allowed to infect social and political order.[2] The rupture of death makes the dead radically other and the city risks destabilizing itself if it leaves the dead unassimilated because this would leave open the possibility that its future involves the continuing production of its radical other.

Elegy, in this context, becomes not only a ritual means of healing rupture but also acts, we might say, as a pass enabling re-entry to the city. It is a personal narrative that guarantees a civic and, by extension, a national narrative. Rose's work underlines the extent to which elegists have been concerned with how to return their dead to the city and extract a use value from them. A few examples are instructive. We already noted in Chapter 4 how Thom Gunn and Mark Doty both sought to return something of value to the city from the crisis of AIDS. We have also noted how Matthew Arnold finds he cannot allow Clough back into the English city. Thomas Hardy's elegy for Swinburne, 'A Singer Asleep' (1910), begins with the poet remembering walking down 'a terraced street' and reading Swinburne's 'new words' for the first time. However, the city's 'brabble and roar' rejected 'thy tunes' so Swinburne has to be located in an imaginary space. Conversely, W. H. Auden imagines Yeats at the moment of death *as* a city that has just had a power cut, and then, in an update of vegetation rites, imagines him 'scattered among a hundred cities' (Auden 1979: 81).

APORIAS AND THE WORK OF MOURNING

The late Jacques Derrida also explored 'activity beyond activity' and the limit represented by death. His later writings became increasingly preoccupied with 'aporias'. 'Aporia' is a Greek word meaning literally the lack of a path or a way through but also a 'puzzle'. In Plato's *Meno* Socrates gives a boy a lesson in geometry that involves calculating the area of a square (Plato 1980: 131–37). Socrates gets the boy to make a guess and then leads him through an argument that shows his guess must be incorrect. The boy becomes confused and this, argues Socrates, is the moment of aporia: when a misconception has been revealed and a space cleared for the reconstruction of true knowledge.

Derrida uses the term to describe both an impasse and a paradox: reaching a point at which one becomes stuck fast in a state of apparent impossibility. He focuses on the paradoxes that underlie practices such as giving, hospitality, forgiving and mourning. These paradoxes take the form of presupposed and accepted limits. For example, if I give someone a gift, I expect them to say 'thank you'. They assume that saying 'thank you' removes any debt to me. However, a genuine gift would require not only absolute anonymity on the part of the giver but no obligations or relationship between giver and receiver. The fact that we choose to act within accepted limits derives from wanting to avoid finding ourselves stuck in an aporia. In the example of the gift, all giving yearns for the absolute altruism of the genuine gift even as it perpetually falls short of it. If every gift becomes a moment of aporia then the act of giving becomes impossible. We make things possible by ignoring the impossibilities they imply.

Derrida's writings on such possible-impossible notions are relevant to the study of elegy because they argue that our conception of death is the aporia that precedes all others. Derrida's argument in *Aporias* (1993) derives from a close reading of Heidegger's formulation of death in *Being and Time* as 'the possibility of the absolute impossibility of Dasein'. 'Dasein' means literally as a verb 'to be there' and as a noun 'existence' but neither correctly translates Heidegger's meaning which is better expressed as 'active being-in-the-world'. The individual's awareness of death as 'something distinctively impending' within his 'being-in-the-world' is what allows him to move towards an understanding of being (Heidegger 1980: 294). This results in 'resoluteness' which is an active embracing of one's own mortality and a decision to live in a way that responds to the inherent possibilities of the active 'being-in-the-world' of one's ancestors (Heidegger 1980: 437, 443). For Derrida, this is an originary aporia because it is at first sight clearly impossible for us to experience our being as defined by something we cannot experience, namely our non-being.

But, as any elegist would point out, we can to some extent experience non-being through the death of others. Indeed, the individual's awareness of death as 'something distinctively impending' within his 'being-in-the-world' is demonstrated by the loss of friends and relatives. At the same time, to return to Abraham Lincoln's Gettysburg address, the dead bequeath us the unfinished business of living, both theirs and our own. The idea of others' non-being leading to our own continuance underlies death's foundational role in culture. Culture, Derrida argues, is 'before anything . . . the culture of death'. Culture 'Consequently . . . is a *history of death*. There is no culture without a cult of ancestors, a ritualization of mourning and sacrifice, institutional places and modes of burial, even if they are only for the ashes of incineration' (Derrida 1993: 43).

Culture, then, is what allows us to experience our own non-being as a condition of our being. This is one lesson of the story of Phocion. Plutarch's account ends by telling us that his death reminded the Greeks of the death of Socrates who was also sentenced to death on false charges because 'the two cases [were] so similar, and both equally the sad fault and misfortune of the city'. The city is here literally a history of death because the deaths of its public figures become the measure of its justice or injustice. The deaths of Socrates and Phocion reveal that justice has a limit in that it harbours a tendency to be unjust. Justice therefore includes the possibility of injustice and, at the same time, shows that human justice will always fall short of absolute justice. The belated burial and commemoration of Phocion within the city represent a yearning for absolute justice and, we might say, a comforting fiction that it is somehow accessible. The story of Phocion and Gillian Rose's reading of Poussin's painting converge with another point that Derrida makes, 'there is no politics without an organization of the time and space of mourning' (Derrida 1993: 45). The decisions about Phocion's death and burial were political acts whereby Athens, as a functioning political entity, rendered itself temporarily inoperative. Decisions about who belongs to the community involve the setting of limits and borders that serve to define a political entity.

Derrida's detailed consideration of death in *Aporias* helps to refocus attention on a number of aspects of elegy. In terms of specific features of the genre, it helps towards a reconsideration of ends. Elegy is the story that starts at the end or, more correctly, that starts with and because of a specific end. The language of the elegist is only possible because the elegiac subject has himself passed beyond language and into silence. An individual speaks and writes because it is no longer possible for another to do so. In the case of elegies for poets, one individual's poetry continues because another's cannot. Elegy is therefore in its own way a species of enquiry into limits and into how to pass through an originary aporia. This, in turn, helps to reveal elegy as an overt dramatization of issues of representability and non-representability that underwrite all poetry. More than any other literary genre, poetry is concerned with looking backwards. Its emphasis on recollection, on the recapturing of particular moments and perceptions, makes it into the writing that can only begin when something else has finished.

Derrida's work in *Aporias* can also be read back into literary studies to suggest that the dominant psychoanalytic turn in elegy criticism over the last 30 years may have resulted in an unnecessary delimitation of the subject. What this delimitation is and how it might be transcended are at the heart of *The Work of Mourning*, 14 texts including letters of condolence, eulogies and funeral orations that Derrida wrote after the deaths of contemporaries such as Roland Barthes and Michel Foucault. Derrida's editors observe that his aim is to 'reinvent ... always from within, a better politics of mourning', and to restore a sense of mourning as 'an impossible performative' (Derrida 2001: 18, 29). As Derrida argues in 'The Taste of Tears' written for the philosopher Jean-Marie Benoist, 'One should not develop a taste for mourning, and yet mourn we *must*. We *must*, but we must not like it ... ' (Derrida 2001: 110).

Understanding and responding to this 'possible-impossible' imperative is crucial if one is to resist and 'shy away from everything in mourning that would turn toward nothingness' (Derrida 2001: 204). The work of mourning is usually characterized psychoanalytically as 'an interiorization (an idealizing incorporation, introjection, consumption of the other)' (Derrida 2001: 159). Derrida's difficulty with this is that we end up losing the deceased, as it were, for a second time. The deceased is acknowledged but then somehow put away and the mourner returns to their everyday life. The truth of the work of mourning is much more complex: the dead go on living 'in us' (Derrida 2001: 159). It is an idea that echoes the poet Stéphane Mallarmé's notes written on the death of his son Anatole in 1879:

> ... so long as we
> ourselves live, he lives – in us
> only after our death will he be – and will the bells of the
> Dead toll for him.
>
> (Mallarmé 2003: 19)

To conceive of the interiorization involved in mourning as a species of afterlife challenges the survivor to be faithful not just to the deceased's memory but to his singularity and alterity. Derrida's fidelity takes two forms. First, the majority of the texts in *The Work of Mourning* quote from their subjects' published works and therefore perform a textual version of the dead's afterlife 'in us'. This is one way of '[keeping] him alive in us, there where he never stopped speaking and writing' (Derrida 2001: 135). Since many of the texts Derrida quotes deal with death their use becomes doubly resonant. Second, Derrida considers non-textual aspects of the dead person's afterlife 'in us': the image and the look. When he writes about Max Loreau's idea 'of writing "hybrid" texts in which "each of two positions ... is in some way contaminated by the other and seen from the other"' he is offering an image of how his own procedure in *The Work of Mourning* goes beyond mere quotation (Derrida 2001: 101). The afterlife of the dead 'in us' can be described and performed in textual terms but our memory of them 'consists of *visible* scenes that are no longer anything but *images*' since the deceased 'leaves "in us" only images' (Derrida 2001: 159). When we look at something, what occurs is an 'inversion of the gaze' so that 'The image sees more than it is seen. The image looks at us' (Derrida 2001: 160). Derrida's reference to 'the gaze' assumes knowledge of both Jean-Paul Sartre's and Jacques Lacan's analyses and uses of the term. Sartre's analysis of 'the gaze' in *Being and Nothingness* (1943) argues that the gaze is what allows me to conceive of the Other as a subject; and my own subjecthood is dependent on the possibility of being seen by the Other. Lacan's conception of the gaze is very different to Sartre's and argues that when the subject looks at an object, the object is always already looking back, but from a point where the subject cannot see it. Where Sartre stresses reciprocity, Lacan, we might say, gives the gaze an existence that is independent of self and other (Lacan 1994: 100–110). Derrida would seem to conflate these two conceptions. What might be termed the reciprocal economy of the gaze that forms the self and the relation between the self and other continues even when the other is no more: 'We are all looked at . . . and each one singularly, by Louis Marin. He looks at us. *In us.* He looks in us. This witness sees us. And from now on more than ever' (Derrida 2001: 161). Death makes the gaze of the other an enactment of his or her 'infinite alterity' which, in turn, because it takes place 'in us' means that '"being-us"' is more than 'a mere subjective interiority' and is in fact 'open to an infinite transcendence' (Derrida 2001: 161). At the same time, in Lacanian terms, that looking back at us takes place beyond our control and emanates from a location that we cannot really see.

Derrida's eulogies and memoirs question the Freudian model their collective title evokes and its assumption that the work of mourning should involve either a reduction of, or a turning away from, the deceased. His own works of mourning imply that Freud's argument that 'respect for reality gains the day' and 'that when the work of mourning is completed the ego becomes free and uninhibited again' is too neat, even wishful (Freud 1917/1984: 253). Freud's elision of the work of mourning with a 'work of severance' is shown to miss the actualities of our continuing relations with the dead (Freud 1917/1984: 265). Derrida seeks a way through the aporia that, William Watkin argues, always faces the mourner: 'To introject the object is, ethically, to deny your responsibility to the object *qua* object in the first instance, but not to introject the object means to leave the object as always, and already lost to us' (Watkin 2004: 188). Derrida's answer is to attempt an introjection or interiorization that remains 'live'. A number of the texts in *The Work of Mourning* end with an emphasis on futurity: in the cases of Michel Foucault and Gilles Deleuze this is portrayed as outlines of imagined conversations (Derrida 2001: 90, 195). Other texts in the volume attempt this 'live' introjection by imagining a return to the start of Derrida's relationship with the deceased. Derrida ends his text for Louis Marin by saying of one of his books 'I feel as if I were still on the eve of reading it' (Derrida 2001: 164). One can perhaps catch an echo of Heidegger's idea that we draw the 'resoluteness' that enables us to continue living from the possibilities inherent in our ancestors' lives. Crucially, Derrida's eulogies and memorial essays help us to see how responsibility to the other in all their difference and uniqueness has become increasingly important to twentieth-century elegists. Derrida's works of mourning also suggest that the Freudian model is inadequate in the emphasis it places on the ego's responsibility to itself.

Introjection that is neither denial nor severance inevitably converges with the ethics of mourning, a concern Derrida shares with philosophers such as Emmanuel Levinas, Jean-François Lyotard and Jean-Luc Nancy. What might be termed 'ethical mourning' shifts attention away from the mourner's journey back to Freudian 'ego freedom' and on to the mourner's responsibilities to the lost other. Ethical, responsible mourning begins with recognition of what Derrida terms 'dissymmetry' and what Levinas terms 'asymmetry'. Derrida defines 'dissymmetry' as the process of introjection that leaves the deceased as 'something completely other' (Derrida 2001: 161). For Levinas, 'asymmetry' is 'the radical impossibility of seeing onself from the outside and of speaking in the same sense of oneself and of the others' (Levinas 1969: 53). We might recall here Derrida's idea of the look of the interiorized deceased that goes on looking back at the mourner. More to the point, Levinas's 'asymmetry' helps illuminate the degree to which canonical elegy relies on the fiction of being able to speak of the self and the other in the same sense. This underwrites the often strained, sometimes ludicrous and generally clumsily idealizing relationships that are figured between elegist and elegized: Seamus Heaney as 'son' to Robert Lowell's 'father', say, or Clough and Arnold as shepherds. It also underlies the way in which many of these poems end with the elegized subject as a ghost or a soul. Lycidas's afterlife as 'the genius of the shore', Thyrsis returning as 'a whisper' and Swinburne's final farewell to Baudelaire's 'silent soul' are of course necessary acts of consolation for the grieving elegist. The deceased has gone to a better, higher existence. At the same time, these poetic afterlives also represent a reduction of what Derrida terms the deceased's 'infinite alterity' to something manageable (Derrida 2001: 161). Portraying the lost other as a ghost or a spirit makes their alterity manageable by transferring it to the realm of the phantasmic and the fantastic.

The ethical turn that would allow death its unmanageability can also be understood as the response of philosophers of Derrida's generation to the Holocaust. In the face of an event where, in Freudian parlance, 'respect for reality' failed to gain the day, the survivor's ego is unable to become 'free and uninhibited again'. In the face of an event so vast, the 'work of severance' is impossible. Survival instead comes to be seen as a privilege. In terms of elegy and mourning, if I were a Holocaust survivor, my coherence and continuance are founded on the death of others. I will always be indebted to others for them. Recognizing this indebtedness is one starting point for responsibility to the lost other. Derrida warns against trying 'to draw from the dead a supplementary force to be turned against the living' (Derrida 2001: 51) in the manner of, say, Shelley's preface to 'Adonais'. Nonetheless, his funeral texts emphasize that while writing about the dead may spring from deep personal emotion, making mourning into a text inevitably makes mourning into cultural performance and cultural work.

THE WORK OF DREAD

Elegy as cultural performance is at the heart of American critic Christopher S. Noble's critique of the work-of-mourning model of elegy criticism. Noble is particularly interested in nineteenth-century British elegists, such as Shelley, Tennyson, Arnold, Christina Rossetti and Hopkins, but his work has implications for the study of elegy in general. Noble's starting point is a re-examination of how Freud's distinction between 'healthy' mourning and 'unhealthy' melancholia has defined the context for most writing on elegy in the last 30 years. For Noble, all elegy criticism and indeed large areas of other writing about death and mourning remain inside the 'rigid boundaries' of Freud's essay and fall into four categories. He goes on to suggest (Noble 2000: 1.7) that this means critics privilege mourning (e.g. Sacks); privilege melancholia (e.g. Jahan Ramazani and some feminist critics); seek some kind of middle position between mourning and melancholia; or seek a middle position while claiming it is radically impossible (e.g. Derrida).

The Freudian account means that elegy comes to be seen as 'analogous to the psychological work of mourning' (Noble 2000: 1.3). In contrast, Noble reminds us that an elegy is not and cannot be structured like the psyche; that Peter Sacks's influential model risks confusing aesthetics and therapy; and that Sacks assumes that, like Freud, 'healthy' mourning involves 'suppression of the death wish and its reinscription in symbolic terms of the father's authority' (Noble 2000: 1.3). What is even more problematic, Noble goes on to argue, is the way that Freud via Sacks has largely set the agenda for critical writing on elegy. Even when feminist scholars have offered detailed critiques of the Freudian model, they have often opposed to it a simplistic counter-narrative of the female elegist 'as a stalwart – dare I say romantic – revolutionary and resister of the father's law' (Noble 2000: 1.4).

Difficulties with and critiques of the Freudian model have already been noted in Chapters 3 and 5. Noble goes further by proposing that the rigid Freudian boundaries of the mourning/melancholia model can be transcended via a new model he calls 'the work of dread' (Noble 2000: 1.8). This is derived from writings by Kierkegaard, Heidegger and Freud. Kierkegaard's *The Concept of Dread* (1844) supplies a definition of dread as 'a sympathetic antipathy and an antipathetic sympathy'. Noble uses this to illuminate mourning as something that both attracts and repels us. From Heidegger's *Being and Time*, Noble takes the concept of *Angst* or anxiety. Anxiety, says Heidegger, is 'completely indefinite' and 'is characterized by the fact that what threatens is *nowhere*'. What threatens us is nowhere precisely because it is everywhere: 'What oppresses us is ... the *possibility* of ... the world itself' (Heidegger 1980: 231). Similarly, 'Anxiety brings *Dasein* [active 'being-in-the-world'] face to face with its *Being-free for* all the potentialities of existence (Heidegger 1980: 232). *Angst* therefore converges with Kierkegaardian 'dread' because *Dasein* involves a similar doubled sense of attraction and repulsion. Noble, however, is more interested in how Heidegger relates 'indefiniteness' to the uncanny and anxiety to the feeling of '"not-being-at-home"' in the world. Anxiety means that 'Everyday familiarity collapses' (Heidegger 1980: 233–34). Noble glosses this so: 'When a person enters a familiar room which is also completely dark, that person is lost and at home in the same instant' (Noble 2000: 1.10). This leads Noble, finally, to Freud's essay 'The Uncanny' (1919) which explores this sense of the familiar becoming unfamiliar in great detail. Noble focuses on Freud's argument that the uncanny involves 'a doubling, dividing and interchanging of the self' (Noble 2000: 1.10).

For Noble, dread comes to mean 'a rhetorical and visual technique' which involves one or all of these concepts. Crucially, Noble's model of dread is what he terms a 'tactical aesthetic' or 'tactical dread' which 'is neither the law nor the rebel, but rather a mode of concealment, a necessary mystification' (Noble 2000: 1.8). 'Tactical' is a key word because it suggests ideas of both rhetorical strategy and cultural performance. The work of dread becomes clearer if we apply it to some literary presentations of mourning. In the funeral procession in Chapter 6 of Charles Dickens's *Oliver Twist*, Oliver, apprenticed to Sowerberry the undertaker, leads the processions in many children's funerals (Dickens 1839/ 1976: 85). Noble argues that phrases such as 'nice sickly season', Oliver's being the object of 'indescribable admiration and emotion of all the mothers in the town', and his having 'many opportunities of observing [the mourners'] beautiful resignation', not only emphasize mourning as a cultural performance but also perform the work of dread. Death inspires Kierkegaardian 'sympathetic antipathy' in that it both attracts and repels us. Similarly, Noble re-reads the famous 'dark house' section of Tennyson's 'In Memoriam' and finds not only 'sympathetic antipathy' in the passage's unstable mixture of 'the noise of life' and the 'ghastly' and 'blank' new dawn but also a refiguring of the house as uncanny, literally *unheimlich* (unhomely). The speaker himself becomes a denizen of the uncanny: 'like a guilty *thing* I *creep*' (emphasis added). Applying Noble's theory to contemporary elegy, we find Douglas Dunn evoking the unhomeliness of the former marital home in *Elegies*: a suspended place of 'waiting' in 'The Butterfly House' or finding in 'Home Again' that 'the room is an aghast mouth' where mouldy grapes drink 'their mortuary juice' (Dunn 1985: 10, 51–52). In the language of 'In Memoriam', death leaves the mourner with an 'unquiet heart and brain'. Elegy transforms this into 'tactical dread' because it must make such unhomeliness powerfully present in order to heal it.

The work of dread facilitates a more detailed accounting for 'the aesthetic constructs that present themselves in nineteenth-century elegy'. It also assists 'the critical potential to investigate relationships between genre and culture' (Noble 2000: 1.12). Such relationships involve 'the representation of private grief [becoming] ultimately responsible for the monitoring of public piety' (Noble 2000: 1.13). This, in turn, means that while the nineteenth century witnessed the return of pastoral elegy, 'the function of the pastoral elements' changed from the signification of the working through of a poetic and psychological process to 'the amplification of the death wish and other apocalyptic elements' (Noble 2000: 1.14). The result is that

> the elegy is about the dread of revelation: like the black mourning veil, it exists to pervade an exterior sense of grief and yet provide for the speaker's specular concealment. It is a show of grief so that grief itself may remain invisible.
>
> (Noble 2000: 1.14)

Further brief examples of Noble's readings must suffice here. His reading of Shelley's 'Adonais' is particularly useful in its focus on the fictionality of the poem and on its culturally performative aspects. He uses Shelley's correspondence to show that the poem had little to do with genuine grief. Shelley only learned the exact details of Keats's death after he had written the poem: 'I do not think that if I had seen it before … I could have composed my poem – the enthusiasm of the imagination would have been overpowered by sentiment' (Noble 2000: 2.8). The real Keats is nowhere present in the poem. The feminized Keats who is present is a necessary fiction: he has to be a weak figure not only in order to provoke our sympathy and justify the out-pourings of the poem but also to allow the speaker of the poem to transcend him and his example. 'Adonais' is therefore an exercise in generic irony that allows Shelley to move back and forth between antipathy and sympathy and the poem's larger structural movements are best understood not as a process but as a series of 'alterations in aspects of its irony' (Noble 2000: 2.8).

The question of who is to be mourned and how are also crucial to Tennyson's 'In Memoriam'. Noting that the subjects of English elegies tend to die abroad, Noble argues that the poem involves 'pastoral problems': how to return English corpses safely to English soil and how to establish the elegist's voice as appropriately masculine. Both problems involve the work of dread. Tennyson celebrates Hallam's paradigmatic English qualities, mourns their loss and fears the consequences of his unfulfilled political poten-tial: 'I doubt not what thou wouldst have been/ . . . A potent voice of Parliament' (CXIII). The poem inscribes 'the political consolation of having Hallam's body buried in English earth' and the dread of 'political instability Hallam's death portends' (Noble 2000: 3.9). The question of an appropriately masculine voice for the elegist inevitably converges with the homoerotic tendencies of canonical elegy which were noted in Chapter 2. Noble argues that in 'In Memoriam' both elegist and elegized are allowed 'a small degree of effeminacy [as] prerequisite to true manliness' (Noble 2000: 3.15). Hallam's 'gentleness' is synonymous, per-haps a little paradoxically, with his bearing 'the grand old name of gentleman' (CXI).

The work of dread, then, facilitates readings of elegy that go beyond the critical model derived from Freud. It reveals canoni-cal elegy as particular species of national work and mourning as an often highly fictionalized cultural performance. Beyond nineteenth-century British elegy, it provides a theoretical frame-work for pondering the exact cultural work done by elegiac writing at particular times. Noble's discussion of how Tennyson and Arnold treat their dead as if they were batteries storing psychic national energy that, respectively, guarantees or threatens the future is especially pertinent. At the same time, so much of the history of the twentieth century and of the beginning of the twenty-first has been, from the Holocaust to 9/11 and 7/7, the history of dead bodies not in their proper places or lost forever. Melissa F. Zeiger argues that 'If the resources of elegy have ... been ... sometimes found wanting, it is partly because elegiac occasions have been so numerous and so dire' (Zeiger 1997: 1). It may also be that the nature of those elegiac occasions has made it impossible for many elegists to conceive of elegy as a renewal of faith in the body politic.

7

ELEGY DIFFUSED, ELEGY REVIVED

ELEGY DIFFUSED: STAYING ALIVE

In offering, in the first two chapters, a history of elegy and an outline of the principal features of the elegiac canon, my intention was to clarify a vocabulary and a usage that have been increasingly subject to revaluation. In following the dominant critical idiom and going on to argue that a genre is at once torturously restrictive and ludicrously leaky, one runs the risk of writing an eternally recurring critical 'fort-da'. Nonetheless, an examination of some aspects of recent British poetry reveals precisely this: a simultaneous presentation and removal of elegy; and the rise of a generalized elegiac mode.

The cover of the first edition of Douglas Dunn's *Elegies* (1985) shows a seated figure reading by a tomb and clearly alludes to Thomas Gray and English pastoral elegy in general. The book's 39 poems use a variety of forms including *terza rima*, blank verse, sonnets, Tennysonian ABBA stanzas and free verse. Its epigraph is from a volume of political verse by the nineteenth-century Italian poet Carducci; and the only overt literary references are to Katherine Mansfield and Pascal. There *are* allusions to elegies by

Henry King and Thomas Hardy but these require expert
knowledge of the genre. Dunn's book clearly exemplifies Dennis
Kay's observation of elegy as 'a form without frontiers' (Kay
1990: 7). The book's plurality and its simultaneous attachment
to and detachment from tradition have other important effects.
Melissa Zeiger argues that much 'current elegiac writing is
intelligibly connected to seemingly remote precedents, and [that]
its own intelligibility depends on those precedents' (Zeiger
1997: 17). *Elegies* does not rely on such intelligible connections.
The plural title dilutes the genre and says that it is both more
available and more necessary. A single elegy is neither uniquely
nor sufficiently powerful. The book's varied forms say that any
poem can be an elegy; that there is more than one way to elegize
and, most importantly, that all poems are potential elegies. Crucially, the book's primary subject is not commemoration of the
deceased but of the poet's own survival of grief.

The idea that all poems are potential elegies echoes the views
of William Shenstone and Coleridge examined in Chapter 2.
Shenstone defined the characteristic of elegy as a 'tender and
querulous idea' (Shenstone 1768: 15–16). Coleridge observed
that elegy '*may* treat of any subject … but always and exclusively with reference to the poet … Elegy presents every thing as
lost and gone, or absent and future' (Coleridge 1835: 268). A
poetry of tender and querulous ideas written exclusively with
reference to the poet is now the dominant mode in mainstream
English poetry, that is, the poetry that is sold on the high street
and rewarded in competitions. Poem after poem ends by reaching
after what is lost or gone as in some random examples from *The
Aldeburgh Poetry Festival Anthology 1989–1998*: 'A bag of pearls,/
that is and always will be far out to sea'; 'before heat goes out of
the day'; 'the fine lines of our lips printed like the claws/of
hungry birds treading lightly over snow'; 'a photograph/he was
unable to stop being developed and fixed'; and 'a lifetime's preparation vanished/into our waiting mouths' (Blackman and
Laskey, eds, 1999: 36, 44, 209, 202, 136).

The similarity of tone throws a well-known habit of contemporary poetry, the negative epiphany, into sharper relief.
Finding its derivation is more complex. It is possible to argue, as

Robert Sheppard does, that such poetry is the result of a 'dominant orthodoxy' based on a Larkinesque 'insistence on poetry as
empirical reconstruction' (Sheppard 2005: 2–3). The mournful
tone of the Aldeburgh examples could be said to derive from
Larkin. However, when discussing a poetry founded on the
recollecting 'I', we should also bear in mind the observation by
Adrian Kear noted in Chapter 1 that identity is itself 'a melancholic structure in that [it] has to repudiate or foreclose those
identifications that enabled it to come into being' (in Kear and
Steinberg, eds, 1999: 183). At the same time, many of the stories in Ovid's *Metamorphoses* remind us that Western literature is
founded on ideas of desire falling short of its object in order for
writing to be produced. Apollo cannot possess Daphne but he
resolves to make the laurel she becomes into 'my tree' so that his
failed desire becomes a species of self-memorial. Similarly, Apollo's loss of Hyacinthus results in the writing out of that loss: 'AI
AI AI, and still the petals show/The letters written there in
words of woe' (Ovid 1998: 17, 231).

The type of English poem we are talking about simultaneously
asserts consistency and integrity and recognizes that it cannot
unconditionally possess the place, event, person or perception it
is using to assert them. The only unconditional possession possible is, paradoxically, loss. In some of the Aldeburgh examples,
things get even more complicated. Pearls that are always far out
to sea, a lifetime's preparation vanishing, or a photograph that
can't be stopped, are actually describing not loss but the impossibility of desire. The poem mourns not lost objects but inoperative desire, desire shut down, desire aborted, desire still-born.
It mourns a lack of desire. Desire and possession are revealed as
another of Derrida's 'possible-impossible' acts. Further levels of
disappointment are also articulated. The orthodox poem aims to
make the impossibilities of existence consumable and tolerable.
This may, of course, in itself be something of a letdown since
the impossibilities of life are usually the very things that make
life worth living. However, the Aldeburgh examples also point
towards or claim to inhabit realms outside language. Since
poetry can only possess things in language, the poet and her
readers are dispossessed twice over. At the precise moment of

claiming to possess the loss of desire, that loss is moved out of reach to a place where, the images of being far out to sea and footprints in snow that will someday melt tell us, it was located all along. In the hopeless finality of such endings, it is hard not to catch a note of self-mythologizing heroism. The poet distinguishes herself by the intensity, eloquence and enthusiasm with which she embraces the lack of desire that has made the objects of that desire valueless or repulsive. Poetry, which always evokes the possibility of transformative encounters, is now always already nostalgic for that possibility. Poetry becomes a celebration of abjection that simultaneously flatters the reader's intellectual vanity and consoles her.

Abjection celebrated and consoled and the marketing of it are visible in the spectacular success of the anthology *Staying Alive: Real Poems for Unreal Times* (2002). The title echoes an earlier, unrelated anthology *Emergency Kit: Poems for Strange Times* (1996) but *Staying Alive* is notable for the way ideas of repair and endurance are developed in the introduction by editor Neil Astley. *Staying Alive* 'is quite unlike any other anthology ... It is a book about what poetry means and how it can help us as people' (Astley 2002: 19). The exact relationship of meaning and help is something that Astley is unable to resolve. On the one hand, 'A poem is not just for crisis' and he takes issue with those who reduce poems to a 'paraphrasable meaning' and use them politically (Astley 2002: 20, 23). On the other, Astley knows that while such arguments are familiar to dedicated poetry readers, they won't interest the 'new readers of poetry' (27) he is targeting. So he focuses on images of poetry as personal crisis management. Poetry can help us with the 'extremes and anxieties in our lives'; is similar to a dialogue with a therapist; and, crucially, can 'make sense of a new age of information and doublespeak, technology and terrorism, of war and world poverty' (21, 23, 24). Astley's 'new readers' are further enticed with swipes at the enemies of poetry such as 'literary theoreticians' (23).

Poetry's life in the world equals help and consolation. Like the majority of poems in Douglas Dunn's *Elegies*, Astley's selection of 500 poems by over 270 writers equates poetry with going on and moving on. In offering poetry as redress for 'a new age ... of technology' Astley reproduces the Victorian view of poetry characterized by M. H. Abrams. The Victorians' clear distinctions between imagination and rationality meant that 'religion fell together with poetry in opposition to science, and . . . religion . . . was converted into poetry, and poetry into a kind of religion' (Abrams 1971: 335). *Staying Alive* updates 'poetry as surrogate religion' for an atheistic age by re-branding poetry as spiritual fix without the inconvenience of having to believe in something first. Crucially, Astley's reference to 'a new age of . . . terrorism, of war' in a book published in 2002 clearly evokes 9/11. An article Astley wrote for *poetrynews* to publicize the anthology makes this even clearer with a reference to 'our new age . . . of indiscriminate terrorism' (Astley 2002: 4). *Staying Alive*'s framing of the poetry in its pages exemplifies several things that have flowed from 9/11 into Western democracies: a nostalgic desire for an age of perpetual crisis; self-justification through the identification of enemies; and a yearning for accessible meaning.

Staying Alive has one more crucial effect: it produces a specific type of reader. In offering 'life-affirming' and 'exhilarating' poetry that is 'help', 'nourishment' and 'redress', the anthology presupposes a reader who is lost, dejected and overwhelmed by a world that appears to be filled with the potential for disaster and punishment (Astley 2002: 19, 25, 24). Such a reader is remarkably similar to the melancholic personality outlined by Freud. He notes that one cause of melancholia can be 'those experiences that involved the threat of losing the object' (Freud 1917/1984: 266). It would not be going too far to say that the anthology's success derives in part from evoking that threat to give the reader the pleasure of a melancholic frisson and the further pleasure of consolation.

Freud also observed that the melancholic 'cannot consciously perceive what he has lost' and, even if he can, cannot perceive exactly what he lost in the lost object (Freud 1917/1984: 254). Such inoperative or incomplete perception is visible beyond the success of *Staying Alive*. For example, it pervades John Ashbery's poem 'Crossroads in the Past' whose speaker is certain that 'something went wrong there a while back' but cannot say what. The speaker decides that what is wrong is 'the beginnings concept' and asserts that 'there are no beginnings, though there were perhaps some/sometime'. He recalls an afternoon cinema outing when 'we didn't fully/know our names' which seems to allude to melancholic failure of self-esteem. The poem ends 'Twilight had already set in'. Its attempt to find an origin discovers only an ending (Ashbery 2000: 76).

ELEGY DIFFUSED: MOURNING HISTORY

Ashbery's poem suggests a double melancholy: that we live after important events and are condemned to keep trying to re-create them. In a discussion of 'the conceptual *and* ethical primacy of melancholy' in contemporary culture, Slavoj Žižek draws attention to what he terms cultish interest in the German conductor Wilhelm Furtwängler (Žižek 2000: 658). He argues that the fascination of Furtwängler's old recordings resides in their 'naïve, immediately organic passion, which no longer seems possible in our era' and in 'a kind of traumatic intensity' deriving from the conductor's determination to protect classical music from Nazi barbarism. The recordings promise Furtwängler's own sense of imminent loss (Žižek 2000: 660–61). The example of Furtwängler highlights not only how culture is increasingly synonymous with memory and the memory of loss but also how such loss is made repeatable. Ironically, what Furtwängler's recordings promise is the sense of an age when music required full attention and could not be conjured or dismissed at the touch of a button.

What needs to be added to Žižek's argument is that any enduring fascination with Furtwängler derives almost exclusively from his relationship with the Nazis. His decision to remain in Germany under Hitler; his belief that art could resist barbarism; the persistent belief that he collaborated with the Nazis even after he was acquitted of such charges; and the subsequent damage to his postwar reputation demand to be read as losses accumulating into tragedy. Our knowledge of Furtwängler starts, like any elegy, with how his life ended. Whether we listen to recordings made before, during or after the war, we are essentially listening to this story. The combination of our knowledge of his life with his performances produces an immediate emotional effect. Furtwängler was himself involved in a work of self-conscious cultural memory. We are able to feel that we are participating in this, albeit belatedly, which may, of itself, increase our pleasure.

The roots of a pervasive cultural melancholy are beyond the scope of this study. However, both Žižek's description of the impossibility of Furtwängler 'in our era' and Ashbery's search for an easily available, stable narrative symbolized by cinema converge with ideas of the end of history prevalent in the last decade of the twentieth century. The idea of the end of history was popularized by Francis Fukuyama's 1992 book *The End of History and The Last Man*, but Jean Baudrillard's view of the same period is more suggestive. Baudrillard argues that the end of history implies 'the resolution of all the contradictions to which it had given rise'. In fact, what we are witnessing is 'the dilution of history as event: its media *mise en scène*, its excess of visibility' (Baudrillard 1998: 8). Such excess, as with endless repeats of news footage of 9/11 and 7/7, negates any sense of a sequential narrative linking past, present and future. We endlessly experience single events as rupture.

At the same time, Baudrillard argues, while the collapse of communism appeared to mark history re-starting itself, 'we very quickly saw that the protagonists of that 'happy ending' had no more cards up their sleeve. So the recycling of history began, we began to live out the film backwards ... ' (Baudrillard 1998: 9). This converges with Baudrillard's observation at the beginning of the 1990s that 'because we have disappeared politically and his-torically today ... we seek to prove that we died between 1940 and 1945' with retellings of Auschwitz and Hiroshima (Bau-drillard 1993: 90). It may well be the case that, to reverse Raphael Samuel's observation, 'Memory began when history faded' (Samuel 1994: ix). The dominance of cultural memory may be one reason why poetry's commemoration of individual deaths has become increasingly timid, indistinct and inoperative. As Melissa F. Zeiger observes 'If the resources of elegy have been ... some-times found wanting, it is partly because elegiac occasions have been so numerous and so dire' (Zeiger 1997: 1). It may also be the case that the complexities of cultural memory require larger forms such as the film.

Two films from the end of the last century underline the close intertwining of elegiac impulses and nostalgia for historical continuity. *Stand By Me* (1986) is based on a Stephen King novella 'The Body'. In a small Oregon town at the end of summer 1959, four 12-year-old boys – sensitive, would-be writer Gordie, 'bad boy' Chris, crazy Teddy and nervous, overweight Vern – go in search of a missing teenager's body. The four get into various scrapes, talk about the future and finally band together to see off the town thugs who are also looking for the body. On one level, then, the film is a rites of passage story but it is also immediately apparent that it is about more than one death and more than one missing body.

The film is told as an extended flashback by the adult Gordie, now a successful author, and is prompted by a newspaper report of the death of Chris, a lawyer, stabbed trying to break up a fight in a fast-food restaurant. The film's beginning with an unseen act of random violence in the present contrasts sharply with one of its key scenes in which Chris and Gordie make steps towards taking control of their futures. Chris encourages Gordie to take writing seriously; and Gordie encourages Chris to enrol for college courses. The story of going to find a dead body is also, then, a story of discovering a sense of self-worth. In Gordie's case, this is lacking because he is 'the invisible boy' as a result of the death of his older brother Denny in a car crash four months earlier: 'my parents still hadn't been able to put the pieces back together'. Denny was his father's favourite and the father's undervaluing of Gordie has become even worse. In another scene, Gordie goes to buy supplies from the local store. The proprietor also makes an unfavourable comparison between Gordie and Denny; comments that the 'Bible says in the midst of life we are in death'; and tells Gordie that his own brother was killed in action in Korea. We also learn that Teddy's abusive father is in a psychiatric hospital, possibly, it is implied, as a result of traumatic experiences in the Second World War.

The film portrays a masculinist culture of death, casual violence and threats of violence between generations of men and boys. The film's quest/mystery narrative, which is underlined by references to 'true crime' magazines and to TV and radio police shows, represents a journey to the underworld and a return from it with insight about the future. The film's portrayal of a death culture is therefore ambivalent. It is clearly nostalgic for a time and a way of life whose continuities were founded on taboo and voyeuristic attitudes to death and violence. At the same time, its setting on the eve of the 1960s suggests that what is also being mourned is the loss of the possibility of progress. Like many canonical elegies, *Stand By Me* begins with a lost body which is then returned to the elegiac city to underwrite its continuance. However, unlike many elegies, the use value of the corpse goes beyond this. The boys set out in search of the body with the hope of being in the local paper or on TV but two of them discover the possibility of transcending the culture whose return the corpse will partially re-energize.

The question of how to return millions of bodies that no longer exist and what form the remembrance of such enormous loss should take are at the heart of Steven Spielberg's Holocaust film *Schindler's List* (1993). The true story of how Oskar Schindler, a Nazi-party member and war profiteer, saved over 1,100 Jews is too well known to need repeating here but its seeming improbability raises a number of interesting questions. When Schindler remarks early in the film that 'that's what I'm good at – not the work, not the work: presentation' he might almost be describing the film's own procedures because *Schindler's List* is predominantly not mourning work. It is, however, profoundly concerned with presentation. It uses a remarkably restrained, documentary style. Black and white photography and unsubtitled German dialogue have the simultaneous effect of distancing the narrative by making it look like an old foreign film and of making its more graphic scenes all the more shocking because they never could appear in such a film. The film's plot also makes clear the extent to which Schindler's own story and the story of the Holocaust involve species of presentation and pretence. For example, Schindler uses Jewish money to buy a Jewish business put into receivership by Nazi race laws and pays his investors back in pots and pans, and the work camps turn out to be extermination camps.

Schindler's List is not mourning work but it is memory work and the film functions in many ways as one of the Yizkor Bikher, or memorial books, that commemorated the lives and destruction of European Jewish communities and were the first Holocaust memorials. As James E. Young observes, the site and activity of reading become a memorial space (Young 1993: 7). A similar thing happens with one's experience of watching the film so that the scenes of thousands of corpses being exhumed and burned make the film into an imagined grave site. However, the film does contain one grave: Oskar Schindler's. In the film's closing sequence, filmed in colour, the survivors, or 'the Schindler Jews' as the subtitle designates them, come to lay rocks and pebbles on his tombstone. The use of colour echoes the film's opening sequence, also in colour, where a pre-war Jewish family light Sabbath candles. They then disappear from the scene like ghosts and the audience watch the candles burn down and go out. The closing sequence has the effect of returning some of the Holocaust's lost bodies in the form of survivors but they gather not at the graves of their ancestors but at that of their saviour. Subtitles tell us that there are fewer than 4,000 Jews left in Poland; that 'the Schindler Jews' have over 6,000 descendants; and dedicate the film to the more than 6 million Jews slaughtered in the Holocaust. The final credits then roll over black and white film of flattened Jewish gravestones. A real, venerated grave gives way to markers of desecrated graves that no longer exist.

The ending of *Schindler's List* is uncomfortable. Hollywood cinema's privileging of heroic individuals means that the film does seem to gesture towards being a species of elegy for one man; and, in Baudrillardian terms, it does seem to mourn an age when heroism could be placed against atrocity. However, I think that the viewer's discomfort comes more from the film's achievement than any questionable focus on an individual. *Schindler's List* successfully walks the fine line between generality and singularity that William Watkin has identified as 'the commemoration conundrum':

> In repeating an event ... does one repeat or does one generalise? ...
> The greatest challenge of an ethical mourning of mass death reveals
> itself to be ... how one can address the dead without reducing their
> singularity through the use of signifiers of summation ...
>
> (Watkin 2004: 230, 231)

The film's focus on what happened to a group of Jews from Krakow has already served to avoid reduction through summation. Less than 4,000, more than 6,000, more than 6 million: the effect of the three numbers at the end is to hold the Holocaust's generality *and* singularity in permanent relation. This is uncomfortable because we are habituated to summation. Summation enables us to shake our heads sadly at some huge number and then get on with our lives. The three numbers at the end of *Schindler's List* do not give us the luxury of putting atrocity away because they take the inconceivable and make it conceivable.

SPECTACULAR DEATH, UNCANNY MOURNING

Schindler's List successfully answers the conundrum of repetition, generality and singularity; and, because it is a film that can be watched again and again, it goes on repeating that answer. In recent years, however, other repetitions of atrocity and mourning have become increasingly problematic. Repeated footage of Princess Diana's mangled car, say, or of the World Trade Center collapsing on 9/11 and the televising of funerals and memorial services for figures as diverse as Diana, murdered English schoolgirls Holly Wells and Jessica Chapman, Pope John Paul II and footballer George Best have produced a new type of public spectacle. As Peter Preston observed in response to media coverage of the death and funeral of footballer George Best, we are all able to line the route of 'the media hearse'. Crucially, such coverage tends to make each event into 'a national moment' (Preston 2005: 28). National identity starts to become synonymous with the performance of appropriate grief and our identity as individuals is somehow validated by the extent of our participation in that performance.

Media coverage and our participation in it exemplify the extent to which our lives are, to borrow the title of Thomas de Zengotita's study of how media shape our lives, 'mediated'. Peter Preston may be right in identifying elements of democratic protest against the establishment in the death rituals of Princess Diana. However, the thousands of people who travelled to lay flowers and teddy bears at the site where murdered eight-year-old

Sarah Payne was abducted in July 2000 revealed another aspect of the response to Princess Diana's death: spectacular death produces spectacular mourning. If both events were 'national moments' then they were so in the sense that, as Andrea Brady has noted in the context of 9/11, 'Nationalism provides an outlet for the individual narcissism repressed in private life' (Brady 2002: 3).

In the context of this study, repeated coverage of Princess Diana's death, 9/11 and the London bombings of July 2005 have other interesting effects. As we have noted, death rituals and elegies culminate in the body being returned to the city. Repeated and repeatable media coverage mean not only that these deaths can go on being enacted but also that the city is changed from the place of return to the place where death is produced. As with roadside memorials, the flowers or wreaths laid at the site of fatal road accidents, the city becomes filled not with graves but with places where people were last alive. In the words of one grieving mother, 'This is where my daughter's spirit was last ... I'm more drawn to this spot than I am even to the cemetery where we keep her remains' (in Urbina 2006: 1–2). The city, then, is no longer the site of last resting places but a place of last moments, of life turning into death. This has the effect of turning what Marc Augé has termed the non-places of modern urban living, the places of transit or fleeting occupation, into uncanny spaces (Augé 1995: 75–80).

The uncanny, as noted in Chapter 4, is used here not only in the Freudian sense of *das Unheimlich*, of the familiar suddenly becoming strange, but in the more sophisticated definition theorized by Rosemary Jackson in her study of fantastic literature. For Jackson, the uncanny is what Heidegger termed the vacancy produced by a loss of faith in the divine, a place 'which is neither identical with God's sphere of being nor with that of man'. Consequently, 'a religious sense of the numinous is transformed and reappears as a sense of the uncanny', that is the realm of myth, magic and the supernatural (Jackson 1995: 65–66). Jackson also follows Hélène Cixous in arguing that the uncanny is unfamiliar and a source of anxiety because it represents 'a rehearsal of an encounter with death, which is pure absence' (Jackson 1995:

68). It represents our terror at the possibility of non-signification. The uncanny, then, is the realm where both individuals and cultures project things that they are unwilling to accept or recognize *and* which are usually repressed for the sake of continuity and stability.

Returning to spectacular mourning, it seems clear that reading public mourning and roadside memorials as either evidence of a wider trend to locate spiritual authority in individual conscience, or a desire to wrest the making of meaning back from organized religion or state institutions, tells only half the story. The city of last moments is the city of deaths left open and of grief forever fresh and raw. In the words of one mourner for Princess Diana visiting London after the funeral, 'I still don't feel as if this is over' (in Balz and Spolar 1997: 3). Indeed, what is striking about the aftermath to events such as Princess Diana's funeral and 9/11 is the idea that it is our *inability* to cope that somehow makes us better, stronger individuals and nations. President Bush made precisely this point in his address at the Pentagon on the first anniversary of 9/11: 'The 184 whose lives were taken in this place ... left behind family and friends whose loss cannot be weighed. The murder of innocence cannot be explained, only endured' (Bush 2002: 1). There is almost no room for the work of mourning here, only endurance: the ability to withstand prolonged strain or suffering. An occasion that one might expect to be a ritual of emotional catharsis was over-written by the language of incomprehension on the one hand and by the language of reaction leading to action on the other. The ritual was rendered inoperative.

Many of the points touched in the preceding paragraphs are thrown into sharper relief by two very different texts: Anne Nelson's play *The Guys* (2002) and C. M. Hopkins's comic novel for teenagers *Holy Moley, I'm A Dead Dude* (2003). *The Guys* dramatizes Nelson's own experiences of helping a New York fire captain compose eulogies for men lost in the events of 9/11. Nelson's two characters, Joan the writer and Nick the fire captain, succeed in their seemingly impossible task but the play also pulls in the opposite direction. The city is the place where, when you talk to people, 'you don't know if they have a God' and where we look at someone and see only their 'public shadow ... We have no idea what wonders lie hidden in the people around us' (Nelson 2002: 20, 39). This incomprehension about others stems from 9/11: 'We can't figure this out. It's too big for us. People used to have religion ... But we don't ... buy that now. God's will? This wasn't God's will. There's no reason. No explanation' (Nelson 2002: 41). And it is an incomprehension that is set to continue. In the words of an offstage character, "'normal will be different. This *is* the new normal'" (Nelson 2002: 56). In a play about the making of writing, this begs the question of what writing, if any, is appropriate. Indeed, the play starts with the irrelevancy of writing and thinking. A friend of Joan's who goes to Ground Zero to volunteer is told 'Plumbers and carpenters first ... Intellectuals to the back of the line'. Joan herself is not a creative writer but a journalist turned editor, someone who has become in her own words 'theoretical' (Nelson 2002: 7, 5). The dramatic effect of a woman who no longer writes and a man who is unable to write producing eulogies is undeniably moving but this emphasis also works to remove the possibility of thinking through and understanding. It is perhaps not surprising, therefore, that the published text of the play is surrounded by the author's 'Preface', a 'Director's Note', an 'Author's Note', an 'Afterword', 'Suggested Reading' and 'Acknowledgements' which collectively assert the play's efficacy in the work of mourning and moving on where the play itself does not.

The city as a place of incomprehension about death and as a fully realized uncanny realm is the setting for *Holy Moley, I'm A Dead Dude*. Dude Harris, guitarist with a successful boy band, is killed at a gig when his famous crowd-surfing stunt goes wrong and finds he has become a ghost in a parallel ghost universe: 'Now, Dude could see the others. Ghosts. Loads of them – different ages, *from* different ages, different races, strolling along, window-shopping, mooching about and chatting to each other as they met up' (Hopkins 2003: 32). With the help of some new ghost friends, Dude finds out that being dead is exactly like being alive only more fun. Ghosts have the same forms they had when they had bodies and the same personalities but can pass through solid objects and surf the internet by scanning themselves into the nearest computer. At the same time, the ghost world has its own particular rules such as no scaring the living without good cause and no spying on girls when they're in changing rooms.

Holy Moley I'm A Dead Dude is a comedy aimed at a relatively young readership but it does reveal some interesting aspects of our view of death. First, ghosts are not privy to any special knowledge. Having an afterlife doesn't mean you know any more about life and death than when you were alive. Grey, one of Dude's new ghost friends, tells him that not everyone becomes a ghost: 'some people go straight through' to another level (Hopkins 2003: 32). There are many levels to existence but no one knows why or when you go up a level. It is just 'like dying in the live people's world' (Hopkins 2003: 41, 37). The afterlife is certainly not a place of ultimate judgement. Second, the plot of *Holy Moley I'm A Dead Dude* turns on interaction between the ghosts and the living. The living can hear and see ghosts 'if they will it' (Hopkins 2003: 37). This makes for some hilarious scenes and some highly sentimental ones. Eventually, Dude learns that ghosts, like the living, have to move on from former attachments although he will still be able to visit and talk to his younger brother and his former girlfriend. Finally, the book takes great pains to explain its ghost world through science: how ghosts exist as HTML on the internet and how they can take on solid form by lining up the electron orbits in air atoms. Hopkins's novel, then, is a curious mix of desire, fear and scepticism. Death, the great unknown, comes to us all – but not really. It is exciting being a ghost but even ghosts pass on to a further great unknown. The ghost world is uncanny but not especially supernatural in any clichéd way and turns out to have a solid basis in science. *Holy Moley, I'm A Dead Dude*, like *The Guys*, seems to articulate our culture's acceptance of how ill-equipped we are to face death and mourning.

ELEGY REVIVED

Spectacular mourning offers us the incomprehensibility of death and suffering *and* the legitimacy of an immediate, uninformed response. The arbitrariness of death is mirrored in the arbitrariness of our impulse to place flowers at a roadside or sign a remembrance book. At the same time, the fact that in common parlance 'everyone can remember what they were doing' on, say, 9/11 means that spectacular mourning is as much self-remembrance as commemoration of the dead. In allowing us to participate in a public performance of immeasurable loss that verges on narcissism, spectacular mourning risks losing the dead altogether. William Watkin raises a similar point in the context of 9/11: 'How to count the dead means also how to group them and divide them and separate them off. I feel our culture is currently unaware as to how to do this ethically' (Watkin 2004: 234). Such ethical inability may derive, as Gillian Rose argues in *Mourning Becomes the Law*, from the impasse of postmodernism. It may also derive from an anxiety that speaking of individual, separate deaths is unethical in the face of the uncountable elegiac occasions of the Holocaust, breast cancer and AIDS.

In this context, the Service of Remembrance given at St Paul's Cathedral on 1 November 2005 for the victims of 7/7 was notable for the Archbishop of Canterbury's emphasis on separation and singularity. Terrorist acts, he asserted, challenge 'the whole idea that we are each of us unique and responsible and non-replaceable'. Each of the dead was 'precious and non-replaceable' (Williams 2005: 1). He returned to this point throughout his sermon using the word 'unique' a total of nine times and ended by emphasizing that the service was to celebrate the dead 'who are remembered in their separate, unique beauty, who remain with us and in us' (Williams 2005: 3). The service also included the lighting of candles for each of the four bomb sites and the lighting of a single candle with multiple wicks by teenage representatives of the six major faiths: Christian, Jewish, Sikh, Hindu, Muslim and Buddhist. This last act in particular seemed to avoid, in Watkin's words, 'reducing [the dead's] singularity through the use of signifiers of summation' by evoking the different communities the victims belonged to and suggesting a number of possible approaches to what he terms 'death's radical unknowability' (Watkin 2004: 230, 229). At the same time, Williams's sermon was very much of its time in its emphasis on the unavailability and perhaps even inadvisability of lasting consolation: 'the trauma of violence, and even more the death of someone we love makes a difference that nothing will ever completely unmake' and leaves a 'sense of injuries that never really heal' (Williams 2005: 1). The celebration of democratic values relies on remembering the rawness of exception.

A similar willingness to engage with questions of separate deaths, the rawness of exception, the dead's singularity and death's radical unknowability is identifiable in a number of recent elegies that distinguish themselves from both the generalized melancholy that dominates much contemporary poetry and from the passing off of anecdotal recollection as elegy. Nonetheless, writing singularity and Williams's unalterable difference and permanent injury as poetry risks pushing representation into the realm of the uncanny. Sean O'Brien's 'A Coffin-Boat – In Memory of Barry MacSweeney' uses several recognizable elegiac tropes and topoi: it begins in darkness, journeys to the underworld ('this copyright Hell') and evokes the Orpheus myth ('You should [not] look back') (O'Brien 2005: 27). An instruction to 'Go on/To the imaginary light' implies that there will be no brightly lit future or transcendence. MacSweeney's mourners gather in a present 'like a hole in the air' and a history that is 'silence and disuse' on a 'non-afternoon' in 'the era of unwork' (O'Brien 2005: 28). The scene of remembrance, then, becomes an uncanny space of non-signification where the mourners' 'account of [their] presence' lists things they didn't do or say.[1] The poem ends by commemorating MacSweeney's 'anger and hurt' and 'the fact of his rage ... tireless/And homeless' which

> ... even now, at the death and beyond, oh yes
> It must carry on dragging its grievances into the dark
> For the want of a nail, of a home, of a matchbox,
> A drum of pink paraffin, anything fiery enough
> To let the man rest by the waters of Tyne.
>
> (O'Brien 2005: 28–29)

The image of unavailable fire again denies us the consolatory figure of the rising soul. There is no elegiac 'use value' to be had from MacSweeney's life and death. Homelessness figures the lack of a context for them to become settled and therefore explicable. MacSweeney's singularity remains forever 'outside'. The poem leaves him as an undead 'other' whose cancelled linguistic representation parallels that he had and continues to have no place in life.

The desire to retain the dead's singularity and a consequent struggle with adequate linguistic representation characterize several poems commemorating the Australian poet John Forbes (1950–98). One of Ken Bolton's three elegies for Forbes, 'Coffee & John Forbes Poem', begins with a witty reworking of Auden: '"he/ became his admirers"/not much of a fate/for you in my case'. The elegist reads Forbes's last book 'in/exactly the place you'd have/ imagined me in'. Allowing the self to be represented by the other is closely linked to a failure to represent the other: 'what *did* he look like/there writing?' The poem leaves Forbes forever the person who 'saw everything maybe/more accurately. I don't know' (Bolton 2006: 76, 77, 78). Similarly, Cath Kenneally's 'For John Forbes 1950–98' remembers something the poet said:

'You were right

about all that Catholic stuff, mate' –
    it had more power to define us
forever than we cared to allow
           (In Bolton, ed., 2002: 35)

It ends with 'a service/I thought you'd loathe, then thought/you wouldn't'. Other elegies for Forbes by Ken Bolton, Peter Porter, John Tranter and Chris Burns focus on the quality of his attention to the world. So, just as in O'Brien's poem for Barry MacSweeney, the Forbes elegies seek ways of keeping their subject's singularity in the world. They seek ways to continue to be unsettled by it. The effect of the poems converges with the quality that Gillian Beer identifies in ghost stories: 'Ghost stories are to do with the insurrection, not the resurrection of the dead' (in Jackson 1995: 69).

Insisting on the insurrectionary nature of the dead has other curious effects. The largely orthodox forms and language of the poems for Barry MacSweeney and John Forbes simultaneously highlight their subjects' singularity and keep it at bay. Mac-Sweeney's rage and Forbes's discomfiting observational wit are let into the poems temporarily but then placed outside any possibility of settlement. MacSweeney will never 'rest by the waters of Tyne' while Forbes is forever a voice heard on a tape or remembered in mid-conversation. Leaving the dead in the realm of the uncanny converges with spectacular mourning: their singularity is made by the poem into a permanent spectacle. The dead poets perpetually return in the manner of fresh tabloid revelations about the life and death of Princess Diana. This enacts closural suspension but of a different order to that identified by Melissa F. Zeiger in AIDS elegies whose subjects make politicized returns to counter society's marginalization of gay lifestyles and the tragedy of AIDS (Zeiger 1997: 108). The elegies under discussion here do not refuse consolation so much as try to avoid doing anything that might set the work of mourning in motion.

STATES OF MOURNING

This book began with Virginia Woolf asking herself in 1925 whether a novel could be an elegy. Woolf's question goes to the heart of the elegist's concern with questions of form and representation. Both Tennyson bemoaning the fact that 'My words are only words' and Jacques Derrida asking how it is possible for the living to describe non-being articulate our feelings of inadequacy in the face of death. At the same time, the contrast between Tennyson and Derrida is highly instructive. Tennyson's anxiety was no doubt genuine but it is also the typical complaint and disclaimer of the successful elegist-to-be. As we have seen, Derrida's approach is more fundamental: if mourning is work, then what sort of work can it be? In this context, Woolf's question looks forward to the growing preoccupations of postwar elegists: What are we to do with the dead? Where are we to put them? The difficulty in answering such questions has led to spectacular mourning in the wider culture and to uncanny elegies within poetry. The unwillingness of twentieth-century elegists to abandon their dead, identified by Jahan Ramazani and others, has been replaced by a desire for the dead to continue to walk among us. Indeed, reading many contemporary elegies, it almost seems as if we need a new generic term for a literature of the undead.

The tendency for late-twentieth-century elegies to become uncanny spaces where the dead's singularity is perpetually reanimated has been paralleled recently by nations asserting their identity and solidarity through the revisiting of old wounds and the imagining of new ones. As this book was being completed during the summer of 2006, the British Home Secretary called for increased public vigilance against terrorism, while the British Prime Minister promised all households would be compelled to carry out a carbon audit to understand their impact on the environment (Toynbee 2006: 27). Such announcements offer no hope of a positive outcome, and promise only continuing threat and unimaginable loss. Consequently, it seems as if the individual is invited to become Agamben's melancholic and live out 'an intention to mourn that precedes and anticipates the loss of the object' (in Žižek 2000: 661). In this context, the study of elegies and the writing of new ones focus urgent attention on how individuals and nations use their dead, and on how to navigate between the private realities and public fictions of loss.

Glossary

abjection   Literally, a state of misery or degradation. Julia Kristeva notes, 'what is abject' is that which 'is radically excluded and draws me toward the place where meaning collapses'. Abjection, she goes on, is 'what disturbs identity, system, order' (Kristeva 1982: 2, 4). The abject, then, involves ideas of the improper, the unclean and death. Abjection is our reaction to a threatened breakdown in meaning caused by the blurring of distinction between self and other or subject and object.

apotheosis   The raising of a person or a thing to rank of a god or to divine status. The highest level of development of a person or a thing.

attachment   The tendency of human beings to make strong affectional bonds to particular individuals. The making of such a bond by one individual to another.

canon   A body of writings recognized by authority. The canon of literature is a body of writings highly regarded by critics over time and deemed worthy of academic study. In the context of this study, *canonical elegy* may be taken to mean a body of poems that includes Milton's 'Lycidas', Shelley's 'Adonais', Tennyson's 'In Memoriam', Arnold's 'Thyrsis' and Auden's 'In Memory of W. B. Yeats'.

consolation   The act of giving or offering comfort, especially in cases of grief or depression.

dasein   The key concept in Martin Heidegger's *Being and Time*. Literally, 'Dasein' means as a verb 'to be there' and as a noun 'existence' but neither correctly translates Heidegger's meaning, which is better expressed as something akin to 'active being-in-the-world'. John Passmore suggests 'Human Existence'.

eclogue   A short pastoral poem usually in the form of a dialogue between shepherds although an eclogue can also take the form of a soliloquy.

elegy   An elaborately worked formal and lyrical poem lamenting the death of a friend or public figure, or offering serious reflections on a solemn subject. Since Milton's 'Lycidas' (1637) the term has usually been used to describe a lament.

introjection The incorporation of an external object into one's own mind so that the functions of the object are taken over by its mental representation. For example, we introject our parents' ideas of good and bad behaviour so that these determine our own.

lack In Lacanian terms, the lack of an object. Allen Ginsberg uses the term 'lacklove' in '*Kaddish*', the poem in memory of his mother, to describe the state of loving someone who is lost.

loss The state of being deprived of something by separation or death. In the context of this book, the loss of a loved object.

melancholia/melancholy Obsolete term for what is now called depression. Melancholia is characterized by self-reproach and suicidal tendencies.

mourning/the work of mourning The psychological processes that are caused by the loss of a loved object and that usually lead to the relinquishing of that object.

object That towards which an individual directs their action or desire. In psychoanalytical writings, 'object' nearly always refers to a loved person.

substitution A withdrawal of affection from the lost object and a re-attachment of affection to some substitute for the object. So, for example, in Ovid's *Metamorphoses* when Pan finds that Syrinx has turned into reeds he makes pipes of the reeds with the comment 'You and I shall stay in unison!' It is important to note that it is the object-as-something-lost *not* the object itself that is replaced by the substitute. Another way of saying this is that the loss is displaced into the substitute.

trope A figure of speech that uses a word or expression beyond its literal meaning in order to give life or emphasis to an idea. Metaphors and similes are species of trope.

uncanny For Freud, the uncanny involves the familiar suddenly becoming alien and sinister. Such radical defamiliarization of the everyday is closely connected with the uncovering of what is usually kept hidden. For Heidegger, the uncanny is the empty space produced by a loss of faith in divine images, a space that is neither God's nor man's. Consequently, religious sense is transformed into myth, magic and the supernatural. Hélène Cixous argues that the uncanny represents our terror at the possibility of non-being and non-signification (see Jackson 1995: 63–66, 68).

Notes

1 Form without frontiers

1 'Uplondysh' is a variant of 'uplandish', common in the sixteenth century in the sense of rustic and uncultivated.

3 The work of mourning

1 I am indebted to Keston Sutherland for this observation. See 'For Carol Mirakove', in *"the darkness surrounds us": American Poetry*, edited by Sam Ladkin and Robin Purves, published as *Edinburgh Review* 114, pp. 186–90: p. 187. The detailed reading of the later Wordsworth passage is my own.

2 For a similar but differently nuanced reading of the fort-da game which does draw on Lacan and argues that Freud 'wilfully misinterprets' the game see Watkin 2004: 163–65.

6 After mourning: virtual bodies, aporias and the work of dread

1 The painting is known by various titles such as *Gathering the ashes of Phocion* – the title used by Rose – and *The ashes of Phocion collected by his widow*. The title used here is that used by the Walker Art Gallery, Liverpool, where the painting is currently housed.

2 We might also note that the idea of 'cause of death' is an attempt to reclaim death for rationality, to deny it recognition as an unavoidable but natural end. Similarly, the change in the legal definition to 'brain death' – as opposed to traditional ideas of the cessation of heart beat and breathing – might also be read as an attempt to extend the compass of rational order. Death becomes a smaller and smaller stage in a process instead of a sudden, radical rupture.

7 Elegy diffused, elegy revived

1 For a fuller account of the uncanny in O'Brien's poetry see my '"The Aftermath of England": The Cultural Politics of the English Fantastic in Sean O'Brien and Patrick MacGrath' in *Manuscript*, 4:1 (Summer 1999): 64–78.

Bibliography

Abrams, M. H. (1971) *The Mirror and the Lamp: Romantic Theory and the Critical Tradition*, Oxford: Oxford University Press.

Akhtar, Salman (ed.) (2001) *Three Faces of Mourning: Melancholia, Manic Defense, and Moving On*, New Jersey and London: Jason Aronson Inc.

Alexiou, Margaret (1974) *The Ritual Lament in Greek Tradition*, Cambridge: Cambridge University Press.

Ariès, Philippe (1976) *Western Attitudes Towards Death: From The Middle Ages to the Present*, London: Marion Boyars.

—— (1981) *The Hour of Our Death*, Harmondsworth: Penguin Books.

Arnold, Matthew (1959) *Poems*, London: J. M. Dent.

Ash, John (2002) *Two Books: The Anatolikon and to the City*, Manchester: Carcanet Press.

Ashbery, John (2000) *Your Name Here*, Manchester: Carcanet Press.

Astley, Neil (2002) 'Publisher Portfolio – special report', *poetrynews* (Summer): 4.

—— (ed.) (2002) *Staying Alive: Real Poems for Unreal Times*, Tarset: Bloodaxe Books.

Auden, W. H. (1979) *Selected Poems*, London: Faber and Faber.

Augé, Marc (1995) *Non-Places: Introduction to an Anthropology of Supermodernity*, London and New York: Verso.

Austin, J. L. (1962) *How to Do Things With Words*, Cambridge: Harvard University Press.

Bailey, Andrew (2005) 'Lodestar, Polestar – i.m. Peter Redgrove', *Poetry Review*, vol. 95, no. 1 (Spring): 38.

Balz, Dan and Spolar, Christine (1997) 'London Still Overwhelmed With Grief', *Washington Post*, Monday, September 8. Available HTTP: http://www.washingtonpost.com/wp-srv/inatl/longterm/Diana/stories/london0908.htm (accessed 8 August 2006).

Baudrillard, Jean (1993) *The Transparency of Evil*, London and New York: Verso.

—— (1998) *Paroxysm: Interviews with Philippe Petit*, London and New York: Verso.

Benson, Judi and Falk, Agneta (eds) (1996) *The Long Pale Corridor: Contemporary Poems of Bereavement*, Newcastle upon Tyne: Bloodaxe Books.

Berryman, John (1993) *The Dream Songs*, London: Faber and Faber.

Betham, Mary Matilda (1797) *Elegies and Other Small Poems*. University of California, Davis: British Women Romantic Poets Project. Online. Available HTTP: http://www.digital.lib.ucdavis.edu/projects/bwrp (accessed 9 August 2006).

Bishop, Elizabeth (1983) *The Complete Poems 1927–1979*, London: Chatto and Windus/The Hogarth Press.

Blackman, Roy and Laskey, Michael (eds) (1999) *The Aldeburgh Festival Anthology 1989–1998*, Aldeburgh: The Aldeburgh Poetry Trust.

Bolton, Ken (ed.) (2002) *Homage to John Forbes*, Rose Bay, NSW: Brandl and Schlesinger.

—— (2006) *At the Flash and at the Baci*, Kent Town: Wakefield Press.

Bowlby, John (1981) *Attachment and Loss*, Volume 3: *Loss: Sadness and Depression*, London: Penguin Books.

Brady, Andrea (2002) 'Grief Work in a War Economy', *Radical Philosophy*. Commentaries. Available HTTP: http://www.radicalphilosophy.com (accessed 8 August 2006).

Bridges, Robert (1987) *A Choice of Bridges's Verse*, London: Faber and Faber.

Bush, George W. (2002) 'Remarks by the President in Observance of September 11th, The Pentagon'. Available HTTP: http://www.whitehouse.gov/news/releases/2002/09/20020911.html (accessed 8 August 2006).

Butler, Judith (1995) 'Desire', in Lentricchia, Frank and McLaughlin, Thomas (eds) *Critical Terms for Literary Study*, Chicago and London: The University of Chicago Press.

Clampitt, Amy (1998) *Collected Poems*, London: Faber and Faber.

Coleridge, Samuel Taylor (1835) *Specimens of the Table Talk of the late Samuel Taylor Coleridge*, Volume II, London: John Murray.

Corcoran, Neil (1993) *English Poetry since 1940*, Harlow: Longman.

Davies, Jon (1999) *Death, Burial and Rebirth in Religious Antiquity*, London: Routledge.

Demers, Patricia (1999) 'The Seymour Sisters: Elegizing Female Attachment', *Sixteenth Century Journal*, vol. 30, no. 2: 343–65.

Derrida, Jacques (1993) *Aporias*, Stanford, CA: Stanford University Press.

—— (1996) *The Gift of Death*, Chicago and London: The University of Chicago Press.

—— (2003) *The Work of Mourning*, Chicago and London: The University of Chicago Press.

Dickens, Charles (1839/1976) *Oliver Twist*, Harmondsworth: Penguin Books.

Donne, John (1973) *The Complete English Poems*, Harmondsworth: Penguin Books.

Doty, Mark (1995) *My Alexandria*, London: Cape.

—— (2002) *Source*, London: Cape.

Douglas, Keith (1987) *The Complete Poems*, Oxford: Oxford University Press.

Dunn, Douglas (1985) *Elegies*, London: Faber and Faber.

—— (2000) *The Year's Afternoon*, London: Faber and Faber.

Evans, Maurice (ed.) (2003) *Elizabethan Sonnets*, London: Phoenix.

Forbes, John (1998) *Damaged Glamour*, Rose Bay, NSW: Brandl and Schlesinger.

Fradenburg, Louise O. (1990) '"Voice Memorial": Loss and Reparation in Chaucer's Poetry', *Exemplaria*, vol. 2: 169–202.

Freud, Sigmund (1917/1984) 'Mourning and Melancholia', *The Pelican Freud Library Vol. 11: On Metapsychology: The Theory of Psychoanalysis*, Harmondsworth: Penguin Books: 245–68.

—— (1920/1984) 'Beyond the Pleasure Principle', *The Pelican Freud Library Vol. 11: On Metapsychology: The Theory of Psychoanalysis*, Harmondsworth: Penguin Books: 269–338.

—— (1991) *On Sexuality: Three Essays on the Theory of Sexuality*, London: Penguin.

—— (2003) *The Uncanny*, London: Penguin Classics.

Fussell, Paul (1975) *The Great War and Modern Memory*, Oxford: Oxford University Press.

Ginsberg, Allen (1987) *Collected Poems 1947–1980*, London: Penguin.

Gorer, Geoffrey (1965) *Death, Grief and Mourning*, Garden City: Doubleday.

Greenblatt, Stephen (1980) *Renaissance Self-Fashioning: From More to Shakespeare*, Chicago and London: The University of Chicago Press.

Gregson, Ian (2006) *Call Centre Love Song*, Cambridge: Salt Publishing.

Gunn, Thom (1993) *Collected Poems*, London: Faber and Faber.

—— (2000) *Boss Cupid*, London: Faber and Faber.

Hacker, Marilyn (1994) *Winter Numbers*, New York and London: Norton.

Hardy, Thomas (1968) *The Collected Poems*, London: Macmillan.

Harrison, Robert Pogue (2003) *The Dominion of the Dead*, Chicago and London: The University of Chicago Press.

Heaney, Seamus (1975) *North*, London: Faber and Faber.

—— (1979) *Field Work*, London: Faber and Faber.

Heidegger, Martin (1980) *Being and Time*, Oxford: Basil Blackwell.

Henderson, Hamish (1990) *Elegies for the Dead in Cyrenaica*, Edinburgh: Polygon.

Hewison, Robert (1988) *In Anger: Culture in the Cold War 1945–60*, London: Methuen.

Hollander, John (1975) *Vision and Resonance: Two Senses of Poetic Form*, New York: Oxford University Press.

Hopkins, C. M. (2003) *Holy Moley, I'm A Dead Dude*, Frome: The Chicken House.

Jackson, Rosemary (1995) *Fantasy: The Literature of Subversion*, London and New York: Routledge.

Kay, Dennis (1990) *Melodious Tears: The English Funeral Elegy from Spenser to Milton*, Oxford: Clarendon Press.

Kear, Adrian (1999) 'Diana Between Two Deaths: Spectral Ethics and the Time of Mourning', in Kear, Adrian and Steinberg, Deborah Lynn (eds) *Mourning Diana: Nation, Culture and the Performance of Grief*, London: Routledge: 169–86.

Kristeva, Julia (1982) *Powers of Horror: An Essay on Abjection*, New York: Columbia University Press.

Lacan, Jacques (1977) *Écrits: A Selection*, London: Tavistock Publications.

—— (1993) *The Psychoses*, London: Routledge.

—— (1994) *The Four Fundamental Concepts of Psycho-Analysis*, London: Penguin.

Levinas, Emmanuel (1969) *Totality and Infinity*, Pittsburgh, PA: Duquesne University Press.

Lilley, Kate (1988) *To Dy in Writinge: Figure and Narrative in Masculine Elegy*, unpublished PhD thesis, University of London.

Lutz, Tom (1999) *Crying: The Natural and Cultural History of Tears*, New York and London: W. W. Norton & Company.

Mallarmé, Stéphane (2003) *For Anatole's Tomb*, Manchester: Carcanet Press.

Markham, E. A. (2002) *A Rough Climate*, London: Anvil Press Poetry.

Middleton, Peter (1992) *The Inward Gaze: Masculinity & Subjectivity in Modern Culture*, London and New York: Routledge.

—— (2006) 'Almost Unreadable: Three Contemporary Elegists and the Poetics of Metaphysical and Emotional Limit', in Kennedy, David (ed.) *Necessary Steps: Poetry, Elegy, Walking, Spirit*, Exeter: Shearsman: 44–52.

Milton, John (1990) *Selected Works*, Oxford: Oxford University Press/Oxford Authors.

Murray, Les (1992) *Collected Poems*, London: Minerva.

Nelson, Anne (2002) *The Guys: A Play*, New York: Random House.

Noble, Christopher S. (2000) '"Behind a Black Veil": Bodies in Mourning, the Rhetoric of Dread, and the Nineteenth-Century British Elegy', unpublished PhD thesis. Available HTTP: http://home.socal.rr.com/victorianwidow/diss.htm (accessed 8 August 2006).

Norbrook, David and Woudhuysen, H. R. (eds) (1993) *The Penguin Book of Renaissance Verse*, London: Penguin Books.

O'Brien, Sean (2005) 'A Coffin-Boat: In memory of Barry MacSweeney', *Poetry Review*, vol. 95, no. 2, Summer: 27–29.

O'Connell, Chris (2005) *Hymns*, London: Oberon Books.

Ovid, (1998), *Metamorphoses* translated by A. D. Melville, Oxford: Oxford World's Classics.

Owen, Wilfred (1983a) *The Complete Poems and Fragments*, Vol. I: *The Poems*, London: Chatto and Windus.

—— (1983b) *The Complete Poems and Fragments*, Vol. II: *The Manuscripts and Fragments*, London: Chatto & Windus.

Parker, Michael (1993) *Seamus Heaney: The Making of the Poet*, Basingstoke: Macmillan.

Philips, Helen and Harvey, Nick (eds) (1997) *Chaucer's Dream Poetry*, Harlow: Longman.

Plath, Sylvia (1965) *Ariel*, London: Faber and Faber.

Plato (1980) *Protagoras and Meno*, Harmondsworth: Penguin Classics.

Plutarch (1959) *Lives*, Vol. VIII, London: Loeb Classical Library.

Potts, Abbie Findlay (1967) *The Elegiac Mode: Poetic Form in Wordsworth and Other Elegists*, Ithaca: Cornell University Press.

Preston, Peter (2005) 'This Circus of Grief has Nothing to do with Best', *Guardian*, Tuesday 29 November: 28.

Puttenham, George (1589/1909) *The Arte of English Poesie*, edited by Edward Arber, London: Constable Facsimile.

Ramazani, Jahan (1994) *Poetry of Mourning: The Modern Elegy from Hardy to Heaney*, Chicago and London: The University of Chicago Press.

Rich, Adrienne (1978) *The Dream of a Common Language: Poems 1974–1977*, New York and London: Norton.

Rose, Gillian (1996) *Mourning Becomes the Law*, Cambridge: Cambridge University Press.

Sacks, Peter (1985) *The English Elegy: Studies in the Genre from Spenser to Yeats*, Baltimore and London: The Johns Hopkins University Press.

Samuel, Raphael (1994) *Theatres of Memory: Past and Present in Contemporary Culture*, London: Verso.

—— (1996) *Theatres of Memory – Volume 1: Past & Present in Contemporary Culture*, London and New York: Verso.

Schenck, Celeste M. (1986a) 'Feminism and Deconstruction: Re-Constructing the Elegy', *Tulsa Studies in Women's Literature*, vol. 5, no. 1: 13–27.

—— (1986b) 'When the Moderns Write Elegy: Crane, Kinsella, Nemerov', *Classical and Modern Literature*, 97–108.

Schiesari, Juliana (1992) *The Gendering of Melnacholia: Feminism, Psychoanalysis, and the Symbolics of Loss in Renaissance Literature*, Ithaca and London: Cornell University Press.

Shapcott, Jo and Sweeney, Matthew (eds) (1996) *Emergency Kit: Poems for Strange Times*, London: Faber and Faber.

Shaw, W. David (1994a) *Elegy & Paradox: Testing the Conventions*, Baltimore and London: The Johns Hopkins University Press.

—— (1994b) 'Elegy and Theory: Is Historical and Critical Knowledge Possible?', *Modern Language Quarterly*, vol. 55, no. 1 (March): 1–16.

Shelley, Percy Bysshe (1973) *Poetical Works*, Oxford: Oxford University Press.

Shenstone, William (1768) 'A Prefatory Essay on Elegy', in *Poems*, London: J. Dodsley.

Sheppard, Robert (2005) *The Poetry of Saying: British Poetry and Its Discontents 1950–2000*, Liverpool: Liverpool University Press.

Silverman, Kaja (1988) *The Acoustic Mirror: The Female Voice in Psychoanalysis and Cinema*, Bloomington and Indianapolis: Indiana University Press.

Smith, Eric (1977) *By Mourning Tongues: Studies in English Elegy*, Ipswich and Totowa: Boydell Press/Rowman and Littlefield.

Spenser, Edmund (1965) *Poetical Works*, Oxford: Oxford University Press.

Spilka, Mark (1980) *Virginia Woolf's Quarrel with Grieving*, Lincoln: University of Nebraska Press.

Stead, C. K. (1964) *The New Poetic: Yeats to Eliot*, Harmondsworth: Pelican Books.

Storr, Anthony (1986) *The Dynamics of Creation*, Harmondsworth: Penguin Books.

Swinburne, Algernon Charles (1982) *Selected Poems*, Manchester: Carcanet Press.

Tennyson, Alfred (2003) *Selected Poems*, London: Penguin Books.

Theocritus (2003) *Idylls*, Oxford: Oxford World's Classics.

Thomas, Dylan (1991) *The Poems*, edited by Daniel Jones, London: J. M. Dent.

Tomalin, Claire (2007) *Thomas Hardy: The Time-Torn Man*, London: Viking.

Toynbee, Polly (2006) 'Britain can still lead the world – on climate change', *Guardian*, Tuesday 8 August: 27.

Urbina, Ian (2006) 'As Roadside Memorials Multiply, a Second Look',*New York Times*. Online. Available HTTP: http://www.nytimes.com/2006/02/06/national/06shrine.html (accessed 8 August 2006).

Van Den Abbeele, Georges (1997) 'Lost Horizons and Uncommon Grounds: For a Poetics of Finitude in the Work of Jean-Luc Nancy', in Sheppard, Darren, Sparks, Simon and Thomas, Colin (eds) *On Jean-Luc Nancy: The Sense of Philosophy*, London and New York: Routledge.

Vincent, Patrick H. (2003) 'Lucretia Davidson in Europe: Female Elegy, Literary Transmission and the Figure of the Romantic Poetess', *Romanticism on the Net*, Issues 29–30 'The Transatlantic Poetess'. Online. Available HTTP: http://www.erudite.org/revue/ron/2003/v/n29/007724ar.html (accessed 8 August 2006).

Waldby, Catherine (2000) *The Visible Human Project: Informatic Bodies and Posthuman Medicine*, London: Routledge.

Watkin, William (2004) *On Mourning: Theories of Loss in Modern Literature*, Edinburgh: Edinburgh University Press.

West, Martin L. (1974) *Studies in Greek Elegy and Iambus*, Berlin and New York: De Gruyter.

Williams, Rowan (2005) 'Sermon given at the St. Paul's Service of Remembrance for the victims of the London bombings, 1st November 2005'. Online. Available http://www.archbishopofcanterbury.org/sermons_speeches/2005/051101.htm. (accessed 8 August 2006).

Woolf, Virginia (1982) *Diary*, Volume III, edited by Anne Olivier Bell, London: Penguin Books/Hogarth Press.

Wordsworth, William (1810) *Essays upon Epitaphs*, reprinted in Owen, W. J. B. (ed.) (1974) *Wordsworth's Literary Criticism*, London: Routledge & Kegan Paul.

—— (1986) *The Prelude – The 1805 Text*, Oxford: Oxford University Press.

Yeats, W. B. (2000) *Selected Poems*, London: Penguin Books.

Young, James E. (1993) *The Texture of Memory: Holocaust Memorials and Meaning*, New Haven and London: Yale University Press.

Zeiger, Melissa F. (1997) *Beyond Consolation: Death Sexuality, and the Changing Shapes of Elegy*, Ithaca and London: Cornell University Press.

Zengotita, Thomas de (2005) *Mediated*, London: Bloomsbury.

Žižek, Slavoj (2000) 'Melancholy and the Act', *Critical Inquiry*, vol. 26, no. 4: 657–81.

Index